I0069210

Hard to believe that Renée is a first time author, the simplicity of the messages, the appropriateness of the quotes, the authenticity of her own story all comes together perfectly to form this very motivational read. This book is a must read for those of us that need confirmation that anything is possible when you apply passion, motivation and the right mindset. You need courage, confidence, drive, curiosity, purpose and a vision of the end goal to unlock the Limitless Leadership in all of us.

Maria Palazzolo, Chief Executive Officer, GS1 Australia

>>

Renée spells out what we all know to be true: real leadership comes from somewhere much deeper than skills and techniques. In this brilliant book, Renée holds your hand through a great series of exercises that will uncover your true purpose and tap into your inner motivation to become a 'Top Fifteen Percent Leader', by leading from the inside out.

Peter Cook, CEO Thought Leaders

>>

Work with Renée in person and she is engaging, energetic, purposeful and strong. And that's just how she shows up in the pages of this book. There are many inspiring leadership books on the market - read them and get enthused, then put them down and forget ... empty calories! Renée won't let that happen to you! She is the real deal and is serious about supporting you to develop limitless leadership. In this book, each concept is explained well, with questions designed to extend your thinking, and space for you to jot down your responses. She leaves no wriggle room for you to read, nod wisely and move on ... Can you afford to limit your leadership?

Corrinne Armour, Leadership Speaker, Author, Trainer

Limitless Leadership

LIMITLESS LEADERSHIP

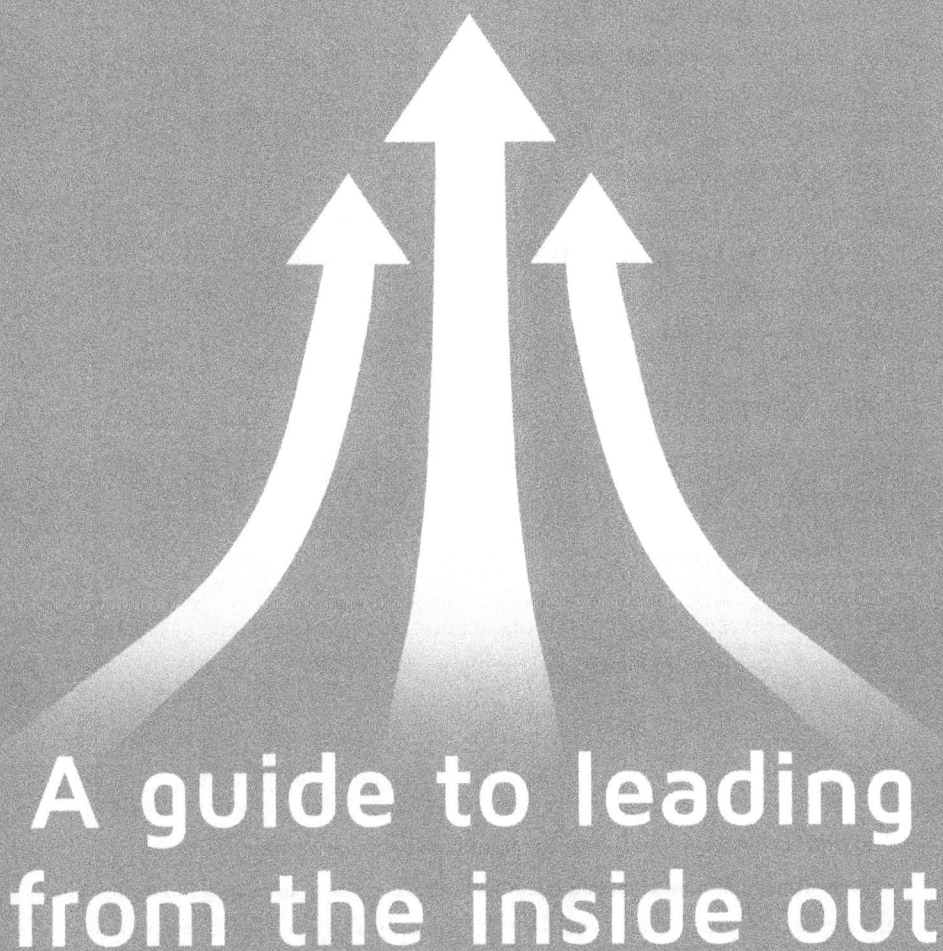

A guide to leading from the inside out

RG Renée Giarrusso

© Renée Giarrusso 2016

First published in 2016 by Baker Street Press | Melbourne

ISBN 978-0-9943214-4-2   eISBN 978-1-925457-28-5

National Library of Australia Cataloguing-in-Publication entry:
Creator: Giarrusso, Renée, author.
Title: Limitless leadership: a guide to leading from the inside out / Renée
Giarrusso; editor: Joanna
Yardley; illustrator: Victoria Brown.
ISBN: 9780994321442 (paperback)
Subjects: Leadership, Self-actualisation (Psychology)
Other Creators/Contributors: Yardley, Joanna, editor; Brown, Victoria,
1989-illustrator.
Dewey Number: 158.4

Edited by Joanna Yardley at The Editing House

Models and illustrations designed by Victoria Brown and copyright of Renée
Giarrusso

Cover design by Cassi Tong

All rights reserved. No part of this publication may be reproduced by any means
without the prior written consent of the publisher.

This book uses case studies to enforce the meaning behind its relevant chapter.
Names have been omitted or changed to protect individual privacy.

Every effort has been made to trace (and seek permission for use of) the
original source of material used within this book. Where the attempt has been
unsuccessful, the publisher would be pleased to hear from the author/publisher
to rectify any omission.

For Mum and Kym who taught me to be brave and fearless, and for Brett, who allows me to be.

CONTENTS

Part Five: Motivation

Part Six: Accountability Vs. Ownership

'We delight in the beauty of the butterfly, but rarely admit
the changes it has gone through to achieve that beauty.'

—Maya Angelou

HOW TO USE THIS BOOK

I wrote this book to encourage reflection. I want to get your thoughts and your leadership juices flowing.

There is a sequence to this book, so start at the beginning and work your way through. Each section layers onto the one before, as your awareness opens up and things come up for you. Most sections in this book contain activities—things for you to do and think about. I encourage you to take the time to complete all activities. Knowing something is one thing, but having a hands-on experience and working through the learnings will assist you in applying what comes up for you throughout your reading of this book.

You need to be fearless before you can be limitless. This book is the first part of being a *Limitless Leader*. You need to lead from the inside out before you can lead those around you. What comes up for you in this book will help you to understand your internal drivers, which will build a solid base for your focus on communication and connection in the books to follow.

Write in this book, tear out pages, or for those of you who are more motivated by procedures and structure you may want to transcribe your insights into a journal, for example, Evernote. This is your adventure, so do whatever works for you. There is no right way to do anything. The 'how' of your 'way' is your choice, as long as it works for you.

You don't have to be leading a team to read or benefit from this book. *Limitless Leadership* can be attained when leading self, decisions and conversations. Having a team to lead is another dimension, but it all starts with self-leadership.

The important thing, and my wish for you, is that you enjoy this journey and take each piece lightly. I want you to invest the time in yourself, no matter what level of leadership you may be at. This is your expedition and you never know where you may end up. Don't make this a burden. It's a light and practical personal quest.

INTRODUCTION

'To lead people, walk beside them. As for the best leaders,
the people do not notice their existence … When the best
leader's work is done, the people say, "we did it ourselves!"'
—Lao Tzu

In my favourite movie, *The Wizard of Oz*, the leading character, Dorothy, is taken on a life-changing journey when she leaves the comfort of her home in Kansas to explore the great Land of Oz. Everything she encounters and everyone she meets is foreign to her and this experience, as scary and uncomfortable as it is, changes Dorothy forever. That is the great thing about change: once it occurs, you can never go back to the way you were.

Dorothy resonates with millions of people the world over as we all move through a fast and challenging landscape of life, both personally and professionally. Dorothy enters Oz on the back of a tornado with the only familiar creature she knows, her dog, Toto. She has to adapt and be open to a new world as she awakens among the vibrant colour and fantasy characters in the Emerald City. Along the way she meets characters that challenge her, scare her, make her question who she is and what is right. She is faced with life-threatening situations where all she has to rely on is her self-belief and conviction in what she needs to do, and why. She has to learn to trust, question everything and take risks in order to get to the great Wizard of Oz who, she believes, will get her back to Kansas.

Throughout the movie, the key characters are all in search of something. The Tin Man seeks a heart, the scarecrow wants a brain and the lion is in search of courage. When they finally reach the Emerald City, they realise they have all they need within them. We are no different; all we need to succeed is within us, we just need to invest in the time to tap into it and bring it to life.

As leaders of teams and organisations, we have more to do and less time in which to make it happen. We are faced with new technologies popping up everywhere we look, complex systems and structures in many of the organisations we work in, and we need to be on top of it all. This is not at all unlike being dropped into the world of Oz.

The United States military is committed to leadership training. It uses the acronym VUCA (volatility, uncertainty, complexity, ambiguity). The key elements of VUCA present the context of which organisations view their current and future state. Volatility refers to the nature and dynamics of change and the speed at which this occurs. Uncertainty relates to the lack of predictability and certainty of change, and this is where our sense of awareness and understanding of issues and events is so important and crucial to our success. Complexity applies to the multiple forces, issues, chaos and confusion that can surround the organisations we are in. Ambiguity relates to the haziness of reality and the mixed meanings of everything we face.

To survive and thrive in such a fast-paced and challenging environment we need to adopt *Limitless Leadership*. But let's first be clear on what leadership is.

Leadership can be interpreted in many ways. Like beauty, its definition is in the eye of the beholder. To me, a leader is three-dimensional. You may be a leader of a team, a leader of self, or someone who leads and influences a conversation or decision. You may be a leader in all three areas. You do not have to have a direct team to be a leader. Leadership can be in anyone; for some it can come naturally—an innate trait—and for others it is a skill that is built upon and strengthened. Leadership is a choice and a decision.

Leadership, and what is means to us individually, needs to be built on, improved, changed and forever evolving—there is no final destination here. It is *limitless*. To reach the top of a mountain doesn't mean we have reached our limit; those who reach the summit of Everest know that reaching the top is only 50 per cent of the equation. After a climber reaches the top, they must descend the mountain. Not only are they physically exhausted and lacking oxygen and focus, they have to bring their entire team down safely—they must believe they can make it back to base. They face uncontrollable variables such as storms, blizzards and high winds. Nothing they face is predictable, so they must be ready for anything and equipped for change. As a leader in an organisation, you are faced with the same challenges enveloped within diversity, technology and structural problems.

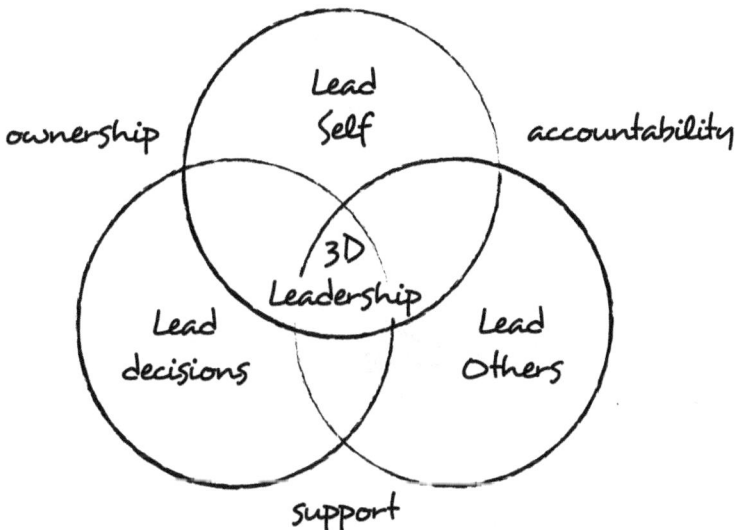

Figure 1: 3-Dimensional Leadership

Limitless Leadership is an ongoing journey. You need to constantly work on, grow and evaluate your commitment, effective communication skills and deep connection with your team, yourself, your organisation and the 'why' of what you do. While this may sound simple, we so often get caught up in the 'doing' and become 'human doings' rather than 'human beings'. Sometimes, no matter what level we think we may be at, we need to step back and observe ourselves as leaders. We need to be an observer of selves by disassociating and looking at who we really are, and where we are really at. By consciously focusing on the three key areas of direction, motivation and opportunity, realisation of where we are at will flow authentically like a natural waterfall—not a man-made version with constant blockages.

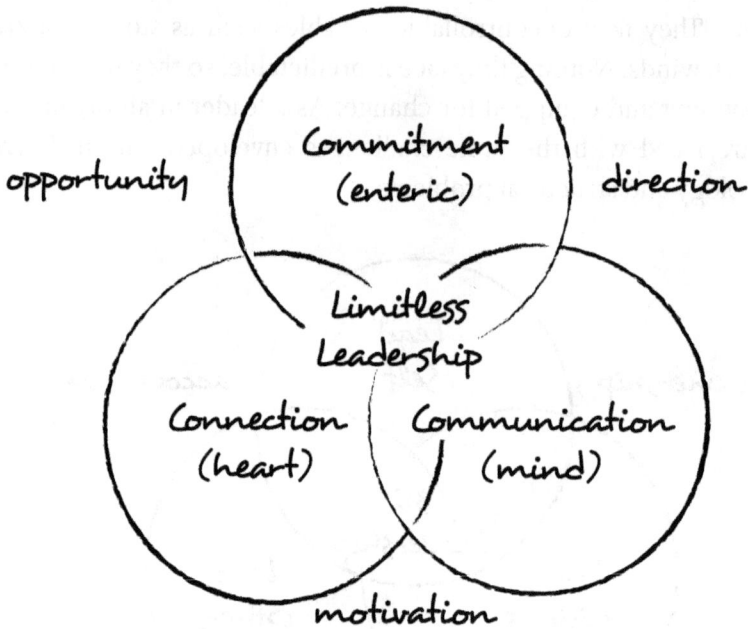

Figure 2: *Limitless Leadership*

Each part of this model deserves its own book. In *Limitless Leadership: A guide to leading from the inside out,* I will be unpacking the piece on commitment. Commitment is a simple word and is often overlooked. It is rarely allocated enough time and reflection for what it really means for you as a leader. 85 per cent of leaders are technically brilliant with only 15 per cent being at the top where they are co-creative, interdependent and synergistic (Rooke & Torbert, 2005). Working with thousands of executives over the last nine years, I have witnessed many technically brilliant people promoted to take on a team, expecting to simply know what to do and excel in a leadership position. An individual may have been a brilliant sales manager, yet when promoted to lead a team is expected to be just as skilled in managing people as they were in selling goods and services. To me, that's like changing careers without support, knowledge and skill in a new area. By applying the *Limitless Leadership* model, we can focus on who we need to be and what we need to do to assist us on this journey.

So what does commitment mean? It is an external behaviour that comes from deep self-belief and conviction in what one sets out to do or be. When I left the corporate world to start my own practice, I knew deep inside what my 'why' was, and that has kept me on track, especially when faced with challenges. I knew that I wanted to grow and assist individuals, teams and organisations to reach their full potential. I literally *felt* this, and that fire still burns in my belly. The day this burning desire to grow and work with others dissipates, will be the day I stop doing what I currently do. Leaving what was a fantastic organisation, great role and guaranteed weekly pay cheque was not without hesitation, but the cost of not doing what I truly wanted was higher than remaining where I was comfortable and socially more acceptable. Now, when I look back, the belief I had in my abilities and skill, and my passion, far exceeded any self-doubt that may have reared its ugly head. I now realise that self-doubt promotes growth, but at the time is not always a pleasant experience. When I left my role, with on-the-job and life experience, I started studying and reading anything that could assist and grow me. I continue to do this, and I reminded myself of all that I have achieved. I use self-doubt as a trigger for further growth. This conviction and self-belief has been imperative to my success. This internal behaviour has built the strong commitment I possess to live my purpose, grow my practice and serve my clients. Commitment can be seen; it is highly visible—clients regularly comment on my level of commitment, energy and passion.

As a leader of self and/or others you need to tap into deep belief of self and purpose, and convert this to a growth mindset that is followed by action, ownership, accountability and, in turn, *Limitless Leadership*.

Get ready to explore where you are at and the places you can go.

Renée Giarrusso

Turning inner potential into outward results

PART ONE

COMMITMENT

TO BE LIMITLESS

'Nothing in life is to be feared, it is only to be understood. Now
is the time to understand more, so that we may fear less.'

—Marie Curie

To be limitless is to break boundaries, knock down walls and false fears, and know in your heart that what you believe you can do is limitless. The word limitless has always resonated with me. Anything is possible and nothing you do has a ceiling, unless of course, you put it there. The minute you limit yourself, you limit your thinking, your feelings; you limit what you need to action in order to achieve what is possible. As babies, we have two fears: a fear of loud noises and a fear of falling. As children, our fears are minimal. We never stop asking 'why' this and 'why' that, and we are endlessly curious of everything and everyone surrounding us. As we grow older, or *mature*, as I like to frame it, we stop asking questions because we fear rejection, judgement and being perceived as inadequate. Then we attempt to redevelop a curious mind not unlike when we were younger. Being limitless in a leadership context means we are forever learning, unlearning, learning again and evolving our thinking and our ways. It never ends—but in a good way. The minute I see people rest on their laurels and think they have hit a ceiling of growth, I get excited to share new ways to innovate and reinvigorate their potential. As leaders, we need to be coachable, teachable and open to take ownership of our growth. How can we grow and develop others if we are not open to growth ourselves? It is a bit like an accountant not taking their own advice or a doctor who is constantly unhealthy.

To become a *Limitless Leader* you need to have true commitment to your leadership through a clear purpose, self-belief and motivation. You need to adopt a bursting mindset—a mindset that is bursting to know, and be more than you already are.

We need to be effective and authentic communicators and deep connectors.

There are six stages or positions we can be at, at any time, depending on such variables as what you value, what you strive for, and where you are at professionally and personally. It is important to remember that each stage is a choice, not a label. It also has a lot to do with your level of self-awareness; in today's society this is often overlooked, and can be dangerous. I want to share what I have seen, what I know and what I believe you can layer onto your journey to ensure the trajectory takes you north on the *Limitless Leadership* ladder.

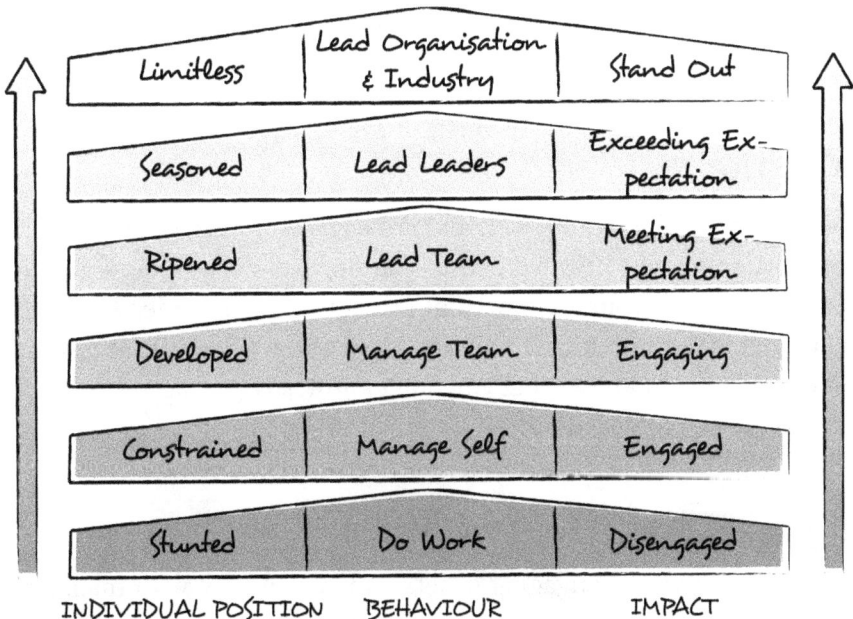

INDIVIDUAL POSITION	BEHAVIOUR	IMPACT
Limitless	Lead Organisation & Industry	Stand Out
Seasoned	Lead Leaders	Exceeding Expectation
Ripened	Lead Team	Meeting Expectation
Developed	Manage Team	Engaging
Constrained	Manage Self	Engaged
Stunted	Do Work	Disengaged

Figure 3: *Limitless Leadership Ladder*

This ladder is simple; it's a great way to gauge where you sit right now and where you want to go and be in the future. You may be near the top now, but this will change when you enter a new role or industry, or take on a new team and new decisions.

Let us have a brief look at each stage of the ladder. You will notice the three columns:

- Individual Position: This simply frames where you may sit
- Behaviour: What are you exhibiting?
- Impact: The consequence of this behaviour.

STUNTED

Here you are doing the work. You have narrow responsibilities, are in autopilot, and are likely to be disengaged to some extent. This is the lowest end of the ladder, where you may be limited in many ways. You are not self-aware. You may be demotivated, just plodding along—your growth is stunted. Here, you only know what you know.

CONSTRAINED

You manage yourself quite well and are engaged to a degree. You may not be running yet; however, what you do, you do well. You are not reaching outside your comfort zone to grow your leadership. Self-management is your focus. You are engaged in what you are doing. Here, you may not know what you don't know, so opening awareness is key to moving up the ladder.

DEVELOPED

You are engaged and engaging others. You are in flow with managing your team. This could be a direct team or indirect reports, even contractors. Your self-leadership is quite strong here. I see many people at this stage, where the progression is to transition from a management mindset to that of a leadership mindset. In this stage, you are still 'in' the team. You are working heavily at an operational level.

RIPENED

Like an apple ready to be picked, you have made the jump from managing to leading. At this stage, expectations are being met in all areas, and there is both accountability and ownership from your end, and that of the team. This is where you are leading. You are empowering and enabling others. You are doing less of the operational-driven tasks and are focused more 'on' the team.

SEASONED

Those you now lead are exceeding expectations under your leadership. You are leading leaders. They are self-reliant; they own what they are doing and you are simply guiding, coaching and facilitating change and progress. You are setting the vision and strategy, and are developing your leadership in order to leverage yourself to lead others and the decisions they need to make. You are acting more strategically and with vision.

LIMITLESS

This is nirvana! Well done if you are here and if you are, you need to work at sustaining this. Although all these stages are obtainable, it is the sustainability to move up and stay there that can be challenging. At this stage, you are leading your organisation and industry. You are cross-functional, co-creative and a strategist. You stand out and continue to grow yourself and those you lead.

Know where you are currently sitting. Be honest. You need to know where you are to know what you have to do to bridge this gap.

This book is one of many that will assist you in exploring where you are, who you need to be and what you need to do to progress towards *Limitless Leadership*. Be open, be ready and be excited to delve in, dissect and build upon all the brilliancy you have within you.

WHERE DO YOU SIT?

'Unless commitment is made, there are only
promises and hopes; but no plans.

—Peter F. Drucker

Do adventure-filled documentaries inspire you to climb mountains? You may think about attempting such a feat, but until you make the decision and take action you haven't committed. Commitment comes after conviction, purpose, self-belief, mindset, motivation, and accountability. Commitment is 'a willingness to give your time and energy to something that you believe in, or a promise or firm decision to do something' (Cambridge University Press, 2016). It is a serious long-term promise, to yourself and others, to dedicate yourself fully to your team, and to the actions you must take to achieve your goals. When committing to anything, especially in challenging times, you need to decide, make a choice and stick to it even when the going gets tough. It's not solely about the promise to do something, it's about investing yourself, boundless effort and action to make things happen. You need to have a sincere fixity of purpose. A committed mountain climber trains, purchases equipment, books annual leave and flights into Nepal, organises a Sherpa, a climbing guide and so on. An uncommitted climber will study it and talk about it without any external action.

Remember, making a decision to be a leader does not mean you have committed. A decision is one-dimensional until there is action.

If you refer back to my story of leaving the safe cocoon that was the corporate world to start my own practice, the real commitment came when I heavily invested in furthering my skills in coaching, speaking, training, then building a website, setting up my practice and leaving my job. Like Dorothy, I burst out of the comfort zone that was my Kansas, into a tornado of change, challenges and uncertainty with no guarantees. This fuelled my commitment even further and afforded me a deep-seated drive to succeed by sharing what I knew by making a difference to others. *When the pressure is on, commitment needs to be strong—those who don't fully commit, look to jump ship.*

Courage and being fearless comes before confidence, and confidence comes before commitment. To lead a team or yourself, and to be believable, effective and authentic, you need to have real belief in what you are doing and why you are doing it. You have to take ownership and be accountable to make it happen. We've all met people who show confidence and self-belief in something, yet fail in action and accountability to see through. It's a bit like turning a dream into a reality. You want the amazing house or holiday; you know all the details, how it looks and feels, but unless you buy the house or purchase the holiday it remains a one-dimensional vision in your mind. You want your leadership to be real and true to you and your team. The model below is a simple overview of what I believe makes up commitment. You could apply this to your leadership or anything you do in everyday life. As we unpack this together, you'll discover you know someone, maybe you, who has been in and at one of the four stages. You cannot work out a path for where you need to go unless you know where you are coming from. Turn on your GPS and it will plot your destination; without it you will drive around in circles.

Let's start with self-belief and accountability as the keys to being fully aligned and committed.

STIFLED

'You're quick to be distracted by worries of mistakes and failing. In short, your self-confidence is nowhere to be found ... Everything is way off and your level of play is just a shadow of your capabilities!' (Goldberg). I liken this to managing a team for the first time; you were technically brilliant in your last role, and now you've been promoted to look after six direct reports. You know the business, you have the knowledge, but right now, your belief in being able to lead a team is as far off as bungee jumping over a waterfall in Kenya. Approximately 85 per cent of leaders are technically brilliant, with only 15 per cent being in, what is framed as The Top Fifteen Per Cent. Those in the top 15 per cent are the individuals who are able to identify specifically where they are in their development stage and engage in skill and personal development experiences that help them move towards increasing levels of competence and influence. It's like they have real-time radar in front of them. In a nutshell, they are highly self-aware.

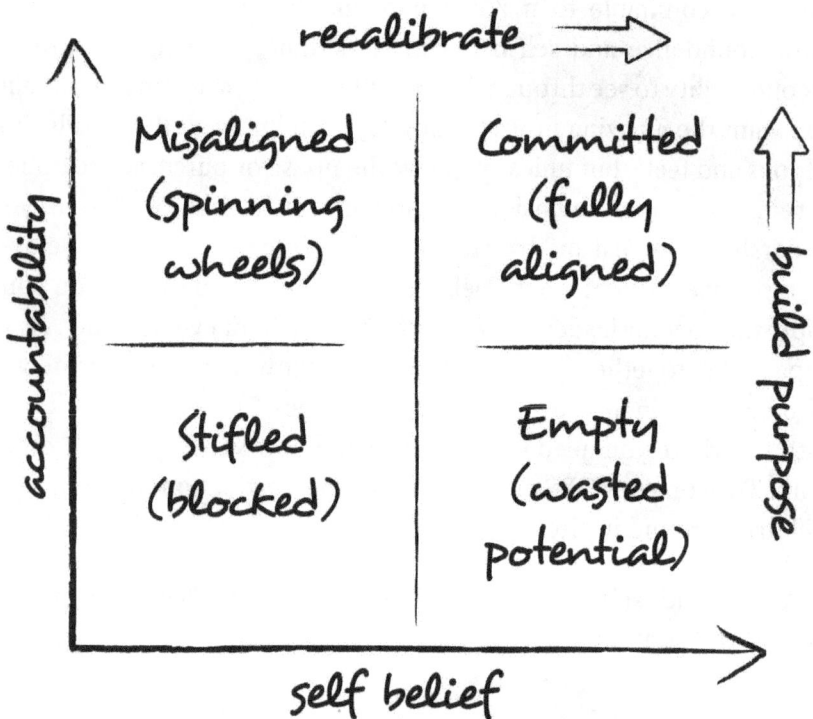

Figure 4: *Commitment Model*

Unless you build your self-belief—and this can be done in many ways— you will remain 'stifled' and may operate in a manager mindset without much success. Doubt is in full force here, but you can transform that uncomfortable and uncertain feeling into growth. Doubt is not a negative thing—it can keep us on our toes but we don't want to be dancing a ballet for long. There is no accountability at this stage as you are blocked from every direction. Maybe you have been here, or maybe you know someone who has or is. If you are here, think about what needs to happen. How can you build self-belief and purpose that will lead to a cadence of accountability? What have you achieved in the past that you can use as a reminder, to yourself, that you can do it again?

EMPTY

Your self-belief cup is full. You know you have what is takes. You have your 'why'. You have a purpose and the courage to lead, but you are not doing the things to bring this to life—your potential is wasted. You are missing accountability. You have taken ownership, which is an internal driver, but have not addressed accountability through actions—the external factors to your success. This is where your purpose may need to be more solid and believable for you to take accountability and move up to the next level. This is where you need to build on your purpose and make it strong and authentic. It's like visiting your *first-choice* holiday destination: you will research it, talk about it, shop for it and be excited when you board that plane. You'd be far less excited if it were your *third choice* of destination. Evaluate your 'why' and purpose here. Do you really believe it with all your heart? If it changed, would you care? Having a strong self-belief in your leadership is great, but you are wasting potential if there is no accountability tied to it. Don't be the firework—the star of the show—that is never ignited. A firework has all it needs within it: a flash card, a fuse and gunpowder. However, its potential is lost if it's never lit up and displayed. How can you take accountability that is aligned with your high level of self-belief?

MISALIGNED

When I think of this stage, I visualise a clown juggling balls or spinning wheels, all of them flying around, falling to the floor, and bouncing and smashing all over the place. There is a mix of colours and a hive of activity and chaos, but no real skill or clarity in juggling them in a sequence or with form. This is where you may be taking action and come across as being accountable but with no underlying true purpose, belief or conviction as to why you are doing what you are doing. In the corporate world, I come across many executives doing a lot of things, but not always the right things at the right time to get the result they were after. Keeping busy and believing you are being accountable with limited self-belief and direction is not a great base on which to build your leadership. It can be a form of self-sabotage or a way to avoid dealing with what is really going on underneath the surface. If you are at this stage, think about who you need to be, and what you need to do to build your self-belief and have real clarity around your purpose. Are the things you are accountable to and for, the right things to drive the leadership direction you want? How is this reflecting on your leadership brand? 'Being' is equally important as 'doing', and sets the direction for success.

> 'In every age there comes a time when a leader must come forward to meet the needs of the hour. Therefore, there is no potential leader who does not have the opportunity to make a positive difference in society.'
>
> —Winston S. Churchill

COMMITTED

You are the firework that is lighting up the night sky. You have deep and real belief in your abilities; your purpose is strong and unshakable, and your accountability is high. You are fully aligned to your purpose and your actions reflect this. You are in tune. Your cadence of accountability is in flow, and you are truly committed. Being at this stage creates a solid base for *Limitless Leadership*, leadership that sees no bounds and is forever evolving, increasing and adapting to the fast-paced and ever changing world in which we live.

You know your purpose, your GPS is set and you have total belief and conviction in the route you have chosen to take. You have your car serviced, destination in mind and are ready for the roadblocks, speed humps and uncharted winds that may be in your path. You have accepted what could go right and have taken into account what could go wrong. You are prepared to be open to, and not be attached to your outcome. Instead, you are ready to learn and grow on the journey ahead. Maybe you are at this stage or maybe you were there once, and something changed. Know your purpose; it will keep you motivated and on track. Once you have reached this stage at any point, you have everything within you to get here again.

When commitment results from deep self-belief, you are on purpose and this, in turn, can build a great base upon which to grow your leadership brand. Yes, you are a brand. You are no different to anything you buy in the market. Remember, people don't just buy products, they buy the person first. In your role, your team, colleagues and internal and external stakeholders buy you before they buy into your ideas, strategy, vision and so on. Think about one of the largest brands in the world, Coca Cola. What does this brand stand for? Whether or not you like its products, the company successfully built a strong brand presence globally and it continues to protect this by continually innovating. A few years ago, Coca Cola launched a one-brand strategy where the name Coca Cola was the umbrella brand with four sub-brands marketed as: Coca Cola, Life, Zero and Diet. Consumers' trust in the Coca Cola brand was so high that this 'one brand' concept was a clear and easy move for existing and new consumers to purchase the new products. The level of trust Coca Cola has built within the market is strong enough for people to gauge their decisions on this and to try to buy four new products.

We have to stand for something and be known for something that aligns with our purpose and that of the organisation or business with which we work. Throughout this book, we will tap into the underlying linchpins and contributors to attaining true and full commitment to your leadership vision. As I mentioned earlier, commitment is one of the three keys to *Limitless Leadership* and our focus of this book. Grab your pen or stylus and jot down where you think you currently sit. If you believe you are in the top right quadrant, that's great, let's look at how you can sustain this in today's challenging and changing world. If you are sitting in one of the other three quadrants, the good news is I am going to give you ideas, tips and thought-provoking activities to help you build your repertoire of go-to tools to keep your commitment on track.

COMMITMENT OVER COMPLIANCE

'One volunteer is worth ten forced men.'

—African proverb

If your team or business is not committed, it can mean a lot of work and 'noise' and usually will not achieve the desired outcome.

Having true commitment in a work context is like having a lamp turned on to full capacity—no dimming or power saving here. If individuals in your team are only *complying*, then the lamp needs to be plugged in and turned on regularly or it will never shine as brightly.

Compliant behaviour is an action or act, and usually has a short-term result that is demanded. Commitment is earned (not controlled) and inspired—it comes from within.

In this book, *you* are the focus, and true commitment has to come from you. Truly committed leaders are 'all-in'. They are not sitting on the sideline because they have to be there. Commitment comes from four areas:

Purpose

As an individual, you need to understand your purpose, the purpose of others and the purpose of your organisation. As a leader, what have you done to share your organisation's purpose, and coach and mentor individuals in your team to understand their purpose and that of others?

Belief

What can you do, with each team member, to instil and build belief in what they need to do and why they are doing it? As a leader, do you have self-belief in what you stand for? Are your values aligned to that of your team and what it believes in?

Motivation

We have internal and external motivations at work. Our external motivators may include incentives, working conditions and our role title. Our internal motivations drive us. What motivates you and those in your team? Do you simply manage these motivations or do you really identify these motivations and satisfy them?

Planned effort

Commitment can occur by knowing what you need to achieve and having the internal motivation and self-belief that you can do it. Knowing is one thing, but action makes things happen. What planned effort are you accountable for? How, as a leader, are you driving this?

Look out for what's not being said, as non-verbal cues can really demonstrate someone's level of commitment. What physiological traits are you exhibiting that demonstrate your commitment? They are easy to see in others. If someone says, *Sure I'll get that done,* with little eye contact, slumped shoulders and no enthusiasm, I would delve into this person's level of commitment.

Take the time to focus on and build commitment within you and your leadership. This resonates strongly with a committed team that will assist in achieving organisational outputs within a happy, productive culture.

PART TWO

PURPOSE

'The two most important days in your life are the day
you were born and the day you find out why.'
—Mark Twain

Over the last few years, there has been a hive of interest surrounding purpose-driven leadership. Research has found that as a leader, knowing your true purpose can lead to exceptional performance, greater health, wellbeing, and clarity in your role as the custodian of the purpose of the organisation where you work. Purpose springs from your identity, and is the essence of your true self. Harvard Business Review published an article that read, '... fewer than 20% of leaders have a strong sense of their own individual purpose' (Craig & Scott A, 2014). I am sure this percentage shocked you as much as it did me. Many people think they know their purpose but can't clearly articulate it. Think of the clearly articulated purpose of Google, '... to organize the world's information and make it universally accessible and useful', or that of Richard Branson's Virgin Unite foundation, '... to unite people and entrepreneurial ideas to create opportunities for a better world'. Both of these purposes are clear, concise and have intent. Purpose is linked to your outcome, where you are heading, why you are doing what you do, and why and where you are directing your team. Don't make the mistake of getting attached to your outcome; be open to change, if needed. A well-achieved purpose has to be *on purpose* or there is no point.

Dr Simon Moss, a senior lecturer in psychology at Charles Darwin University, has extensively researched *purpose*, and his findings conclude that when people experience a sense of meaning and purpose, they become more responsible, resilient, and rational.

He discovered that those who have a sense of purpose and meaning resist immediate temptation and react with less impulsivity. Having a sense of purpose and meaning enables them to embrace unpleasant emotions required for development, so they grow to be resilient (Moss, 2009).

To propel you forward as a leader, you need true purpose connected to your core values, so you can lead and act with accountability, become fully aligned and move on from the 'stifled' and 'empty' quadrant we worked through in the last chapter.

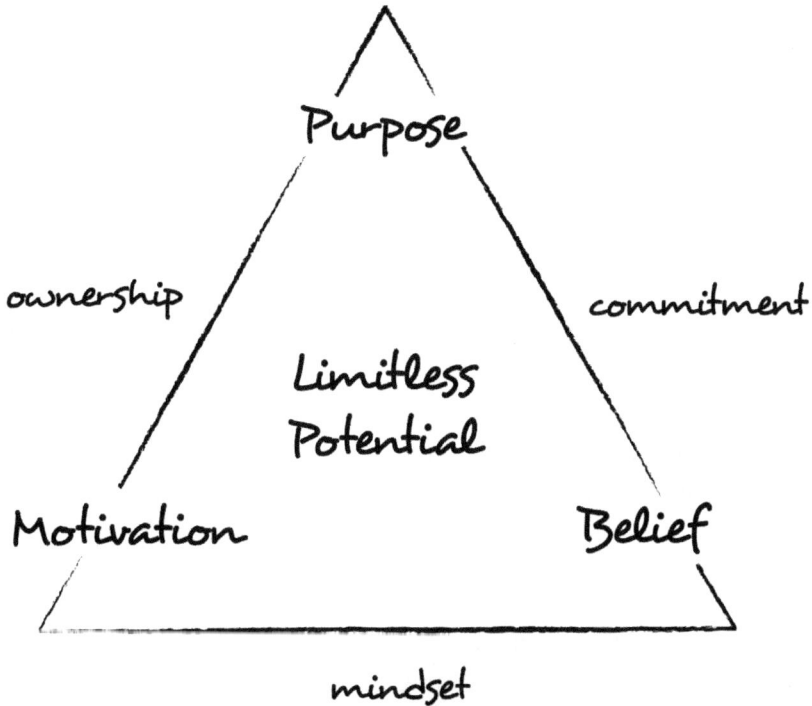

Figure 5: *Limitless Potential*

WHAT DO YOU VALUE AND WHAT DO YOU STAND FOR?

'The great thing in this world is not so much where
we stand, as in what direction we are moving.'
—Oliver Wendell Holmes, Senior

You have heard the saying, *If you don't stand for something, you will fall for anything.*

When taking on a leadership role, you need to make a decision—leadership is a decision. Setting boundaries is imperative. You need to decide who you are as a leader, what you stand for and what you don't.

Take the time to know and authentically believe in the vision you have for your leadership and decide on what you need to give up, introduce and ramp up. In order to commit from the heart, you need to decide the direction for you and your team and for whom you are going to be leader when you show up.

Your character is the essence of who you really are, and you need to allocate time and effort into building your character and what you stand for. Your reputation is the perception of what others think of you. Too often, I see leaders focus on reputation alone and not the heart of which they really are—their character. Character comes from within; it is internal, and I believe is built by you. Factors that make up your character include the ethics you hold, your values, your morals, your integrity. All of these things take time to build. Your reputation is external to you and can be built very quickly, as it is based on the perceptions and opinions others have of you. Others, not you, determine your reputation—it is out of your control. I am a firm believer that we should focus on the things we can control. So take some time to understand your true character, what you believe in and stand for, and focus on this.

Knowing *what* you stand for swiftly illuminates what you *won't* stand for; therefore, assisting you to focus on more of what you do want. This sounds simple, but many of us struggle with it (in and out of the work environment). Saying *no* to people has always been challenging for me. I love to help and be there for others but I have learnt there is a price to pay for this. In my case, that may mean little 'me' time, toxicity from others and a diluted focus on what is important. These elements can impact your mindset, and your physical and emotional health. I have learnt to say no more often by realising that I am saying no to the event, not the actual person. Separating this in my mind has lessened the challenge. In my line of work, there needs to be a cut-off. In order for me to sustain the pace and energy of what I do, and how I serve my clients, those around me and myself, I need to be consistently aware of what I do and don't stand for.

In a leadership role, no matter the size of your team, the decisions you make or the projects you lead, you need to be clear on what you stand for. Being true to this can cascade through your team—the potential leaders of the future. What will it cost you not to lead the future leaders of your organisation? Knowing your purpose and that of the team and business can assist in creating clarity around this.

Identifying your values can be a great conduit to understanding your boundaries. Simply put, values are things that are important to us. We all have values that determine our everyday decisions, from where we bank, to what car we drive, to whom we allow into our inner circle. Values are the underlying linchpin to every decision we make, both personally and professionally. We usually aren't consciously aware of these despite the fact they drive our decisions and our life choices. Values change, and by being aware of what they are we can gain a better understanding of why we feel how we feel when our values are challenged, and when they are met. As children, we gain a large portion of our value set from our parents. As we go through our teenage years, we challenge these values. This is because we are exposed to new values through school, friends and new experiences. These new values may conflict with the ones of which we were once so proud.

For me, this caused conflict between my parents and I during those teenage years. (Sorry Mum, Dad and Kym.) When in a position of leadership, awareness of what you value can assist you to create your beliefs and focus around what you stand for. We can only be clear about our direction by having core values in place.

'Make your work to be in keeping with your purpose.'
—Leonardo da Vinci

Some of you may remember Apple's classic 1984 commercial that was played during the third quarter of Super Bowl XVIII. In the commercial, there was a huge focus on the establishment of personal computing. Apple cast itself as the hero, who, in a rebellious way, launched into the dull and grey landscape of the working world to save employees from the stagnant computing manufacturers that led the market.

Apple's mission statement back then was, 'To make a contribution to the world by making tools for the mind that advance humankind (Mission Statement, 2009)'. In 1984, Apple had only a small percentage of the personal computing market but the vision, which told a compelling story about changing the world, had already reined in many fans. *Your* vision will be determined by what you value and what you are willing to stand for as a leader.

Values have characteristics within them:

Energy:

Our values are the energetic force behind our actions and decisions. They carry weight and determine the way we live our life, whether or not we are consciously aware of this.

Priority:

Our values do not carry equal weight. The context, situation and the environment decide the order of priority. You will have a preference to rank values depending on what they mean to you.

We tend to rank our values in order of importance to our team and us.

Conflict:

Values can compete for the top spot to assist our decision-making—especially in challenging situations. This is why we can sometimes feel torn when making a decision or we may sit on the fence when deciding, and not really know why.

Changeable:

Values are chosen early in life. We need to be aware that values can change as we change, and they always will, depending on situations, experience and those around us.

Impact:

Values can create impact, and by communicating values at work this assists in building trust and rapport.

Working out what you stand for can seem a bit daunting, especially if you have never explored this before. Let's be honest; how often do we sit down over a coffee and reflect on what we value? Let me make it easy for you. Here is an exercise I've performed with many teams and individuals, to nut out what is really important to them at an individual, team and organisational level. It is a great exercise to do as a group (team). You can brainstorm what values you want to live by, decide on the top five or six and rate them on a scale of 1–5 as a way to formulate an action plan for which the team is accountable. Monitor, reformulate and align with the organisational values as an ongoing task.

1. Make a list of eight things that are important to you: creativity, family, growth, freedom and so on.

1.		2.
3.		4.
5.		6.
7.		8.

2. In the first column below, write down eight things you don't stand for ... that's right, the things that you believe are totally incongruent with who you are. These could include being stifled, uncreative, directionless. Then write down the opposite word for each item.

Things I don't stand for	Opposite
Example: *Decline*	*Growth*
1.	
2.	
3.	
4.	
5.	
6.	
7.	
8.	

3. Work through your list and circle all the opposite words. You now have values that you do stand for.

4. Compare your Values you do stand for list to the first list you created (the things that are important to you). Take time and cluster these

words into groups until you have at least 5–6 key values with which you are happy. These need to resonate genuinely with you. If they don't, rework them until they do.

My core values are growth, family, collaboration, passion, honesty and contribution. I tap into my core values every few weeks. I simply rate them on a scale of 1–5, with 5 being *I am living this value to the fullest* and 1 being *this value is missing in totality*. You can do this too, and then after you have rated them, choose the lowest three and ask yourself: What do I need to do, and who do I need to be, to dial this towards a 5?

This will create an actionable plan you can execute and check in on to ensure you are leading based on what is important to you and what is strongly linked in with your purpose.

YOUR 'WHY' TO BE LIMITLESS

'Be the change that you wish to see in the world.'
—Mahatma Gandhi

Does your 'why' for change exceed your 'why' to stay the same? Does your energy spent on change exceed your energy spent trying to remain the same?

Working with hundreds of leaders over the last decade has given me amazing insights into how individuals deal, or not, with change, particularly when changing their belief of self and others.

Many people, in a management or leadership position, like to be known strong and effective leaders. They continually ask me, *How do I get there?* or *What do I need to do?*

The answer is different for everyone. There's no magic pill or solution. It's a discussion around what is working and what needs to change for them as individuals, as well as within their team or organisation.

For many of us, making a change or dealing with change thrown upon us does not come easily. Reasons for this can include fear of rejection, failure and uncertainty. As human beings, we tend to focus on what we can't change as opposed to what we can. Understanding your 'why' and linking this to your purpose is a great starting point for building self-belief.

Thinking about things you want to change—how you lead your team, having coaching conversations with your team—cause noise within your mind. What could go wrong? What will happen if I look incompetent? What if it doesn't work? This noise will continue until you know your 'why' *for* making the change, which needs to exceed your 'why' for *not* making the change.

For instance, many organisations are becoming more coach centric, and for good reason. The most effective organisations have leaders who conduct coaching and mentoring regularly with their teams. When leaders encourage and lead coaching conversations with their staff, it not only empowers people to think for themselves, it saves time in managing behaviour, ensures less 'surprises' as feedback is ongoing, and creates an open and trusting environment for development.

I'm sure you would agree that the 'why' for this is strong. Conversely, if a leader is not open to focusing on what the change will bring, it won't occur, and conversations with staff will be more 'telling' type conversations, which will address none of the above.

Three points to consider when making a change

1. **Know your 'why' for the change**
   - Why has this idea for change come up?
   - What are the benefits for addressing this?
   - What will the change look like?
   - What do you want to achieve for yourself and the team?

2. **What is drawing you to make the change?**

   - What will you see, hear and feel once the change is in place?

   - What won't you see, feel and hear?

   - What are the key things pulling you towards this change?

   - What energy do you have to make this change?

3. **What is holding you not to change?**

   - If nothing changes, how will this look?

   - How will you feel if nothing changes?

   - What will it cost you to not make this change?

   - What will be the outcome if nothing changes?

When what is *drawing* you *to* change has more energy than what is *holding* you *not* to change, it's time to take definitive action. Remember, if your energy isn't directed towards the change, revaluate this and what you need to do to make it happen.

'LINK & SYNC' YOUR PURPOSE

'And the day came when the risk to remain tight in the
bud was more painful than the risk it took to blossom.'
—Anaïs Nin

Think of a car. Any car. Like all cars it was engineered and manufactured to be driven and enjoyed, and to get its owner from A to B. Now imagine this car sitting in a closed garage for an infinite period. It just sits there; it's never driven. The car doesn't care; it could sit there forever. But what if the car had a soul or a conscience? If that car were abandoned for days on end, it would feel the impact. It would feel strange inside, lonely, probably useless and off centre. (I know cars don't have feelings, stay with me on this one ....) One day the garage door opens and the owner walks in. She or he opens the driver's door, starts the ignition, adjusts the mirrors and puts their seatbelt on. The car is suddenly awoken and flooded with potential and enthusiasm. It is doing what it was made to do—and it feels good.

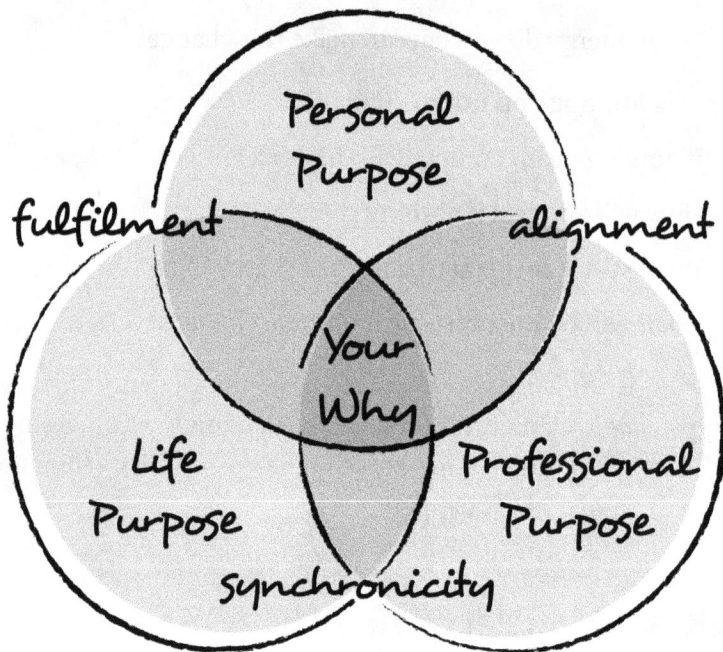

Figure 6: *Purpose Model*

As humans, we are no different; we have an innate purpose, a reason for being.

Our purpose can change, it can go off track, and it can sometimes be hidden, but it is always there. Many of my executive clients ask, *How do I know I'm living my purpose?* The answer is only **they** can know this. Finding your passion in what you do and knowing your 'why' is the key. As a leader, you cannot be fully committed if your purpose is not clear, believable and true to you. The organisation you work in has a purpose to which you need to align your greater purpose and the purpose of your team. Purpose gives you direction, a meaning to what you need to do and, therefore, should be congruent with what you value.

Purpose comes from within, and there are three areas—buckets, if you like—of each type of purpose which needs to be filled. These buckets obviously need to be aligned, there is no point doing what you love professionally and travelling to the point you are never home, if your personal purpose is to enjoy and be there for your family. Each bucket needs to 'link and be in sync', so each one can flow into the next with ease.

It all comes down to finding out what you are passionate about and what lights you up from the inside. Here is an exercise to help you identify purpose in various areas of your life. Take some time to answer the questions below. This will give you alignment, fulfilment, satisfaction and ideally synchronicity within all the areas in your life. Be mindful that your purpose can change as *you* grow and change.

Personal Purpose

What is it you stand for?	
What don't you stand for?	
What legacy do you want to leave behind?	
What lights you up?	
What do you believe in?	
What is important to you, for you?	

Professional/Leadership Purpose

What are you passionate about, in the organisation you work within and for yourself?	
If you could do anything in your role, what would that be?	
What part of your role do you love the most? (Don't confuse this with what you are good at.)	
What would success look like as a result of your role in the next 12–14 months?	
How does your role motivate you?	

Life Purpose

What will you want others to say about you once you have moved on?	
What do you care most about in your life?	
What legacy do you want to leave behind?	
For you, what three words sum up a life well lived and 'on purpose'?	
What excites you?	
What sparks your creativity?	
What contribution will you make?	

From a leadership perspective, I absolutely loved my corporate roles. I couldn't do what I do today if they hadn't been part of my journey. It wasn't until I started running my own practice nine years ago, where I grow and develop individuals, teams and organisations, that I realised that I am truly living my purpose—to make a difference, learn in the process and help people grow and reach their full potential.

I work hard, I travel, I'm continually studying and growing my knowledge, and as tired as I may get I always feel lit up, excited and passionate about what I do to the point most clients comment on my energy—they can see I love doing what I do. This deep-seated clear purpose keeps me going when times are tough and keeps me committed to my goals, my clients and being the best version of myself as a thought leader.

So how do we identify what we are passionate about? Too often, we hold ourselves back from the things we want to find out most. We fear it could change us, change how we do things or how others perceive us.

We make excuses about what could change or we simply don't take the time to seek out what is important to us. We get caught up in the 'doing' not the 'being.'

The questions below will provoke some thought into discovering what you are passionate about and how you can contribute these to your commitment as a leader:

- What sparks your creativity?
- What lights you up and gets you excited?
- What puts a smile on your face?
- What do you find easy?
- What things, activities, experiences, places, talents, problems and ideas do you love to think about and work with?
- If you looked back on an ideal year, what would have happened?

Having a clear idea of your purpose and linking and syncing each area of purpose in your life will assist you greatly in being motivated and focused. You will be able to tap into this pool of energy whenever challenges arise. This is because you now understand the 'why' behind the events in your life, both professionally and personally.

LEAD SELF TO LEVERAGE PURPOSE

'Action springs not from thought, but from
a readiness for responsibility.'
—Dietrich Bonhoeffer

Limitless Leadership needs us to self-lead and take responsibility. After all, you would have to agree that responsibility is our ability and ownership to respond. We need to choose this. We need to be agile, accountable and responsible for the results we have created and will create. Leading self before others can be the real game changer where we see teams and individuals flourish.

We become a mirror of this as our team becomes a mirror of our leadership. We need to be 'at cause', which means we will be in a position and mindset to be accountable for the results and situations we produce.

A strong purpose is like building the foundation of a house, there is no point putting up the frame if the base is unstable or non-existent. The house may look great aesthetically but if the base is not solid, in time the walls will crack and the floors will sink. Likewise, in the movie, *The Wizard of Oz*, Dorothy's purpose is to get home and her focus on this is unwavering. As much as her friends deviate from the Yellow Brick Road along the way, they end up back on track through Dorothy's strong purpose to reach the Emerald City. *You have to lead with a clear purpose of self before others will follow you.*

Take the time to know and grow your purpose and what you stand for. Only then should you communicate them to your team. In my corporate days, I helped pioneer a new sales channel. It was one of my favourite roles, not just because it was a dynamic, greenfield role with unlimited possibilities, but because in setting up the channel, and the roles within it, I had no choice but to have a clear purpose and be self-led to get it to that next stage. Only when it became a full-fledged channel operating profitably (with a team), did I realise how important it was that I had my purpose and the purpose of the team in place before the team started. We don't always get the opportunity to start a new channel but we do get the chance to clean the slate and recreate our purpose and lead ourselves in the best way we know how. By doing this, we are in a position to lead self, lead people and lead the organisation, in that order.

The executives with whom I work all have one thing in common: a lack of time to lead themselves and others. This is a sad reality. It can cascade to future leaders within the business.

If leaders aren't self-led or leading a team, *truly* leading a team, what are they doing? We can combat this dilemma by working across the three levels a leader needs to be at to stay on purpose and leverage their time for balanced leadership.

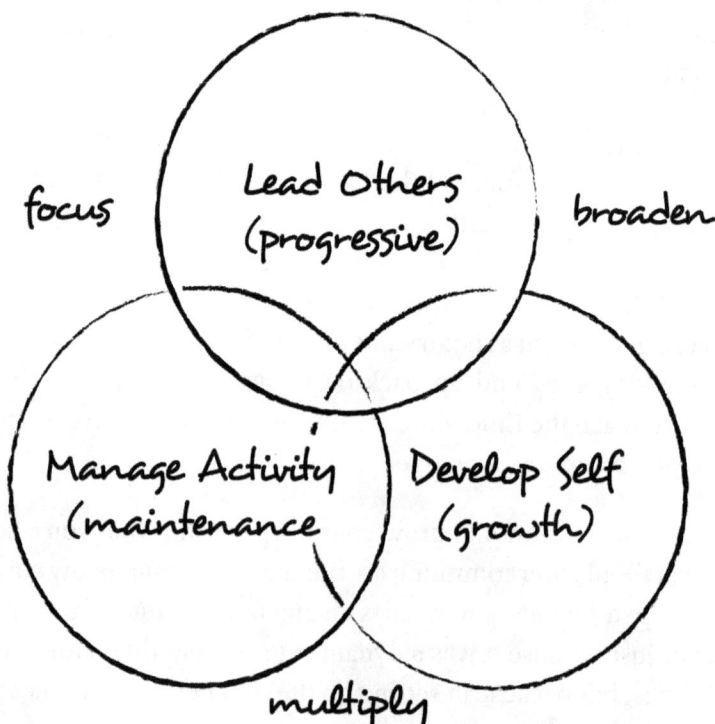

Figure 7: *Lead Self to Leverage Purpose*

Progressive: Lead others

These are leadership-based initiatives such as setting vision, creating strategy, coaching your team and running workshops. These things build your leadership and are 'on' the team not 'in' the team.

These initiatives could contribute to your legacy as a leader and should be generated from your purpose and the purpose of the organisation. If you aren't in a formal leadership position, this area is all about leading self and growing self. Leading others or self includes progressive tasks. A progressive task at home could be renovating your house or building a new deck—an addition as opposed to an everyday task like cleaning the house, which has to be redone regularly.

Growth: Develop self

Choose activities that can develop you as leader and further develop you in your current and future role. You may consider joining an industry association; attending a workshop; reading relevant material; or being coached/mentored on your leadership or current role, if you are self-leading. The world is your oyster when it comes to personal growth. There are limitless webinars, books, podcasts, workshops and seminars at your fingertips. This area links in nicely with the 'progressive area', as what you learn you can share and contribute, thereby increasing your leadership or expertise in the role. I have witnessed people who invest time and focus in this area flourish, and let go of a manager mindset and adopt a leadership mentality, which serves them and their team well.

Maintenance: Manage activity

Activities here could include writing and running reports, performance management, attending and running meetings. These are the day-to-day operational tasks that need to be done but at the same time could be minimised if delegated effectively. This is where your focus is heavily working 'in' the team, not 'on' it. Unless you free up time by reallocating a few things in this area, you will never have the time or head space to grow progressive tasks that are the core of your leadership and spend time developing yourself.

Here is an exercise I recommend doing every 4–6 weeks to keep you on track and to ensure you are doing the right things at the right time so you get to live your purpose and build on your leadership brand.

Use the following table to make a list, based on what you currently do, under each of the three areas. If you do not currently lead a team simply circle self in the first column heading.

After you have exhausted each area, you will notice what area is overflowing. I usually see the maintenance column (manage tasks) overflow, as many of us get caught up working in the team and not on the team. What can you delegate from the maintenance area to shorten this list and free up time to spend in the progressive and growth areas? This is simple, although not always easy to do. A conscious ongoing focus on this will keep your 'why' and purpose on track.

Lead team/self	Develop self	Manage tasks

Lead team/self	Develop self	Manage tasks

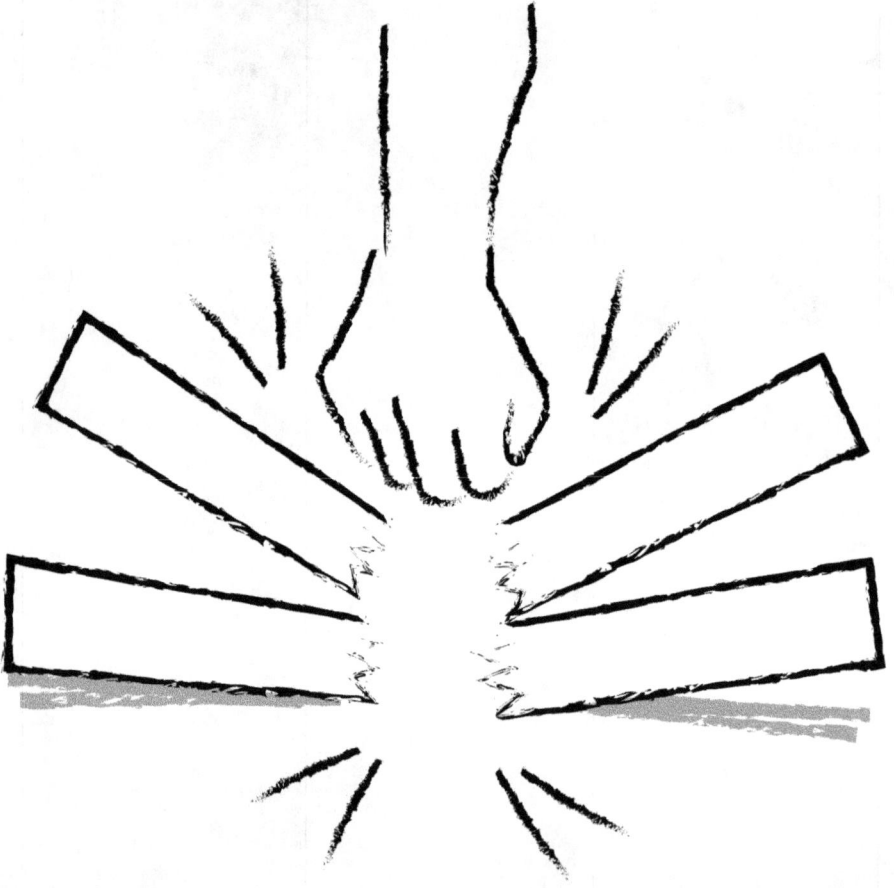

PART THREE

SELF-BELIEF

'Here is a test to find out whether your mission
in life is complete. If you're alive, it isn't.'

—Lauren Bacall

A newspaper editor fired Walt Disney because, 'he lacked imagination and had no good ideas' (Horowitz, 2011). After numerous bankruptcies he went on to build the first ever Disneyland, even after the first park in Anaheim was rejected. Van Gogh only ever sold one painting in his lifetime, and that was to a sister of one his friends for a measly $50 in today's currency. He still went on to paint over 800 masterpieces. These are common stories. What if they had given up? What would we be missing out on today? Mickey Mouse and the characters of Fantasia would not exist and would not have lit up the hearts and minds of children the world over. JK Rowling authored a book about a young boy wizard that was rejected by 12 publishers before a small London house picked it up. I would have been devastated, being a devout Harry Potter fan, if this mythical tale had not made its way into my world.

So what do all the people in these stories have in common? They didn't give up—no matter what the cost. They had a strong belief in themselves and their ideas and dreams. They were tenacious and had a clear purpose to which they were fearlessly committed. Highly successful people have a strong commitment to action; they don't need to question what they believe to be true. Beliefs are lies we tell ourselves. Beliefs are things we consider true. They form the basis of our thoughts and influence the choices we make. Beliefs change, they come and go. What about Santa Claus? There was a time it served us to believe in him. Flexibility in our beliefs doesn't always come naturally. Beliefs become stronger with time and reinforcement. I see executives with deeply held beliefs they find hard to shake. We subconsciously focus on information consistent with our belief and it builds this muscle, this belief. This is because our cognitive system will do what is necessary to preserve these beliefs.

To lead in today's world, you can have the best intent and a golden purpose, but without belief in yourself and the journey ahead, you will remain one-dimensional. You need to adopt courage before confidence and conviction to believe in yourself and your purpose.

TURN SELF-BELIEF INTO TRUE CONVICTION

'Be sure you put your feet in the right place, then stand firm.'
—Abraham Lincoln

Conviction derives from self-belief; this alone is a personally held belief. It is internal and leads to commitment. It is what the world sees and what you project as a leader.

I think of conviction and belief as inwards and commitment as outwards. Conviction happens on the inside along with self-belief, while commitment is what we see and feel on the outside. Belief is a mindset. As a leader of self and others, you need to choose the thoughts that give you the emotion to be excited and sure of yourself.

Our beliefs are based on our personal position, which is a result of many contributing factors. These factors include our experiences, culture, values, upbringing, biases and ultimately our map of the world and how we view it. We all have our own view of the world—our imagination. The magic we see or don't see depends on who we are, where we came from and what key influences have shaped us and shape us. If we were all flying in a plane over a vast green field some of us would see grass, some a field, some would only see the pond. The fact is, we all see what we want to see based on our perspective. There is no wrong or right, just what is to us.

If what we see, feel and tell ourselves doesn't serve our greatest good then we need to let them go. You need to believe authentically in who you are and what you are doing as a leader. Clear purpose, congruency of values, direction and passion will assist in increased confidence and belief within yourself. When self-belief is authentically ignited and projected, others cannot help but believe in you.

'Go confidently in the direction of your dreams.
Live the life you've imagined.'
—Henry David Thoreau

- What are you doing to ignite your self-belief even further?

- If your conviction to your beliefs was a colour, do you need to turn up the vibrancy?

  » Is it mauve and needs to be bright purple?

- What is going on between these two tones of colour?

Many of us are unaware of our own beliefs. They are not on our radar and we don't think about them or question them consciously. Invest in the time to map out your beliefs. Remember, beliefs are what we tell ourselves, usually over and over again. The more attention and thought we give them, the more real they become. You need to make sure your beliefs serve and empower you. If they don't, you can rewrite them.

Take some time to dissect and discover your beliefs around your leadership.

What do you need to believe in, from the heart, to be the truest and best version of a leader you can be?

In the following model, you will see that to have true conviction in your beliefs you need to have two things: an alignment with your values and a highly driven self-belief.

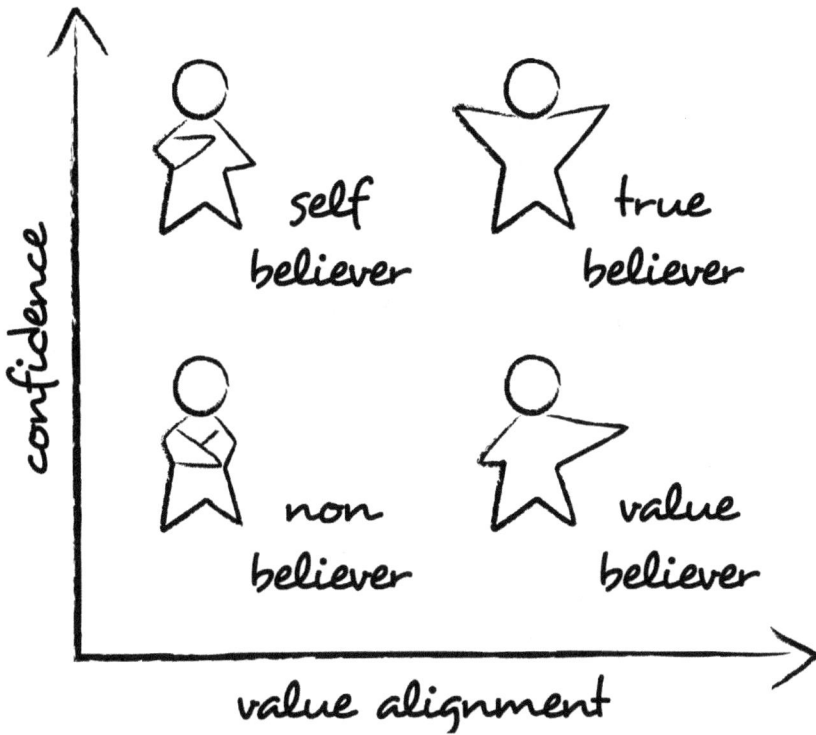

Figure 8: *True Believers*

This model outlines an easy way to navigate where you think you might currently sit. Along with a strong purpose, you now need to unpack where you sit by looking at the level of belief you have in yourself and the level of alignment your values offer to support this.

The **Non-Believer** sits in the bottom left quadrant. Here your values aren't aligned with your purpose and plan, and you have little or no belief in them or yourself. To move up to *true believer* status, you need to revisit what you value and align these elements to your purpose to build real, deep and true self-belief.

The **Value Believer** has strong alignment of values to their purpose but no belief in themselves. If you are at this stage, you need to identify what beliefs are limiting you, flip them to serve you and your purpose, and link them into the values with which you are already aligned.

The **Self-Believer** emits and has strong self-belief but little or no value alignment to their purpose. Values need to be identified and aligned here to get you to *true believer* status.

The **True Believer** has high self-belief and alignment of values to his or her greater purpose as a leader. This is the superstar quadrant. To remain here, make sure you revisit what you value as the purpose may change, and always keep in check with the beliefs you are holding. Make sure there are no dead cats hanging around to prevent you shining as bright as you could be.

Use the following exercise to document two beliefs that do and don't serve you as a leader. See how you can flip those beliefs to move you forward.

Check in by using the True Believers model to keep on track and ensure you have limitless conviction in what you believe.

1.
2.

Write down two beliefs that don't serve you as a leader:

1.
2.

Flip the beliefs that don't serve you to ones that will empower you moving forward:

1.
2.

BREAK OUT OF THOSE RUBY SLIPPERS

'At the moment of commitment, the entire
universe conspires to assist you.'
—Johann Wolfgang von Goethe

To build self-belief you need to break out of your comfort zone. Your comfort zone keeps you safe, but there is no growth there.

Is every day easy? Do you feel no stress? Do you have no real drive for anything? If the answer is yes, yes, yes, you are in that bricked-up circle known as the comfort zone, a safe haven that surrounds you. I know people who live entirely within their comfort zone. They stay in the same house for years or live in the same area; they stay in the same job and visit the same holiday destinations year after year. Nothing much changes for them. If they are happy in this zone, I say *good on them*. These same people comment on how much I have done and achieved and they sometimes say, *I can't believe all the things that happen to you and all the things you are doing.* My mind ticks over. It wants to reply and say *Well of course things happen to me. It's inevitable when you put yourself out there.* One of my top five values, as I mentioned earlier, is growth; so taking risks, welcoming change and constantly moving, evolving and embracing uncertainty are high on my list of priorities, and to date this has served me well. Whether you are a leader of self, a leader of others or you are in a position of influence to lead decisions and change, you need to shake things up and get outside your zone of comfort.

By looking at the beliefs that limit you, you are looking outside what keeps you safe and comfortable. A bit like Dorothy when she is dropped into the Land of Oz, away from everything and everyone she knows as she awakens to a vastly uncomfortable next chapter of her life.

As she gets used to the Land of Oz and becomes inseparable from her acquaintances, she is now back in a comfort zone but outside the initial one she lived in back in Kansas. She is given a pair of ruby slippers from the Good Witch of the East, where she can tap her heels anytime to go home and yet she doesn't utilise these powers until she reaches her end goal of getting to the great Wizard in the Emerald City. Just like reframing our beliefs to serve us this can initially feel uncomfortable, weird and clunky, once we get used to new ways we are back in comfort land. Awareness of this and keeping in check on what we need to do and who we need to be is vital in ensuring we break through the many circles that surround us. Not unlike a cross-cut piece of timber the circles keep going and going, but by breaking through each one there is growth. I want to look back on my life and see numerous circles I have broken through, as every breakthrough is growth.

To break through, stop focusing on what you need to do; your purpose will guide you here. Instead, be still and think about who you need to be. It doesn't matter what you do to achieve what you want, unless you are not being who you need to be first and foremost to make it happen. We have all heard that person say, *When I have the money I'll buy a big house and have a holiday and then I'll change jobs and be happy.* This is wrong on so many levels. It's great to start with the end in mind but who do you need to be, day in and day out, to fuel your actions to achieve your plans? Reflecting on who you need to be right now is vital. It will help you break out of your comfort zone.

Shaun, a senior leader, was extremely busy working **in** his team, not **on** it and, therefore, had no time to create and lead strategic vision for his team and organisation. He was working night and day, totally burnt out. This was not only affecting his health but also his emotional and spiritual wellbeing. He was too busy to attend some of his mentoring sessions with me, which was a sure sign that something needed to change. A light bulb moment occurred when we worked through where he was at and discovered, together, that he was using procrastination as a strategy. By keeping busy, he had no time to stop and be who he needed to be. Instead, he was doing the wrong things at the wrong time and, therefore, the results weren't anywhere near where they needed to be. Shaun was clearly in a comfort zone; this was safe and easy, and like a train on an express route, he made no time to stop and get off at each station to see what was really going on. He wasn't even aware of what he valued or the beliefs that were driving him. After delving into this, at a deep level, we worked through what he valued and who he needed to be. This resulted in some profound insights. He needed to be present, strategic, focused and purposeful. These four words then changed his beliefs around what he needed to do. Yes, he had to bust out of his comfort zone, but the payoff was huge.

What will it cost you, your team and your organisation if you do not break through your safe zone?

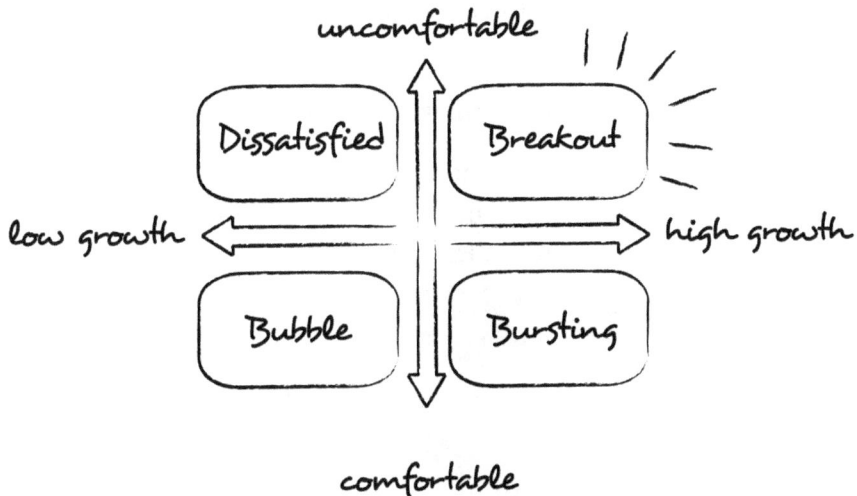

Figure 9: Break out of those ruby slippers

A bit like going from a risk-averse investor who prefers lower returns with known risks, Shaun is now working from a place of higher results/returns with unknown risks. Shaun and his team's performance, morale and direction has increased since he embraced uncertainty and learnt who he needed to be rather than what he needed to do.

Who do you need to be to live your purpose both professionally and personally?

What do you need to let go of to live *who* you really are? What beliefs do you need to instil and what ones do you need to bury and rewrite? The following exercise will help you decipher who you need to be to live your purpose. Take some time on this. Aim to understand fully where you are at and what needs to change or be slightly tweaked. Many teams put this activity into play as a group or one-on-one.

1. In the first column, write down *what* you would like to have or believe in to be the best leader you can be.

2. In the middle column, list all the things you need to *do*, the actions you need to take.

3. In the last column, brainstorm who you need to *be* to achieve this.

Focus on the last column as you apply this back on the job, and who you are being day in and day out. This is vital as a focus and will flow on to action and achievement (the WHAT and HOW).

What	How	Who

STRIP BACK CONDITIONAL THINKING

'Since everything is a reflection of our minds,
everything can be changed by our minds'
—Gautama Buddha

When looking to fully commit as a leader, don't add more thought than necessary. Instead, strip back conditional thinking and see what comes up. Conditional thinking is like a habit, the more we think about something, the more life we give to it. Think of a child, who, for years, was told they were no good. If they hear this enough, the thought forces them to look subconsciously for reasons and evidence that they are no good—both internally and externally. This in turn creates a self-fulfilling prophecy I call our *inner spiel into real*. What is real is what we make it, which is great news as we all have the freedom of choice and thoughts that dictate our actions.

As solid as your purpose and intent may be, if you don't strongly believe in it and strip back the thoughts that trigger you to hold back, there is no way you can move forward. Your thoughts are connected. If you have a clear intent to project a message to your team, but in the back of your mind you don't believe in that message, no matter how passionately you convey this, it won't come across as authentic.

Building a strong belief in yourself and your purpose is vital. If you are having doubts, there can only be growth ahead. Doubt is not a bad thing; yes, it's perceived as a negative feeling or emotion and it requires us to reconsider and feel uncomfortable, but with all challenges comes growth.

Instead of trying to pursue happiness actively, while trying to avoid negative emotions, we should go the other way and look towards negative experiences and embrace the learning inherent within them (Fox, 2015). Dr Jason Fox believes there are three key benefits of doubt. These include:

1. Doubt makes ideas stronger: By being a fundamental piece to all discovery, learning and growth, it causes us to question things that can lead to great breakthroughs. Doubt births wisdom.

2. Doubt makes leaders better: How often do you compare yourself to colleagues and others and have felt that sooner or later they will realise you are not as smart as people think you are? This is called the imposter syndrome and occurs when we compare ourselves to talented peers. It is where we compare our own internal perception with the confident facade others project on us. As this syndrome actually gets worse, we become better. So in doubting yourself, you are probably doing really well (Burkeman, 2013).

3. Doubt makes life more wonderful: By not thinking about things in binary terms where there always has to be a right and a wrong, you can look at things where nothing is conclusive. There is no need to take sides on a decision or a thought. This changes your perspective and behaviour and opens the space to wonder. By letting go of certainty and the need to be right, you can be open, curious and embrace doubt and the opportunity to grow and learn.

Doubt causes us to question things and in turn awakens us to new possibilities and ways of thinking. This propels us out of our comfort zone or default way of thinking and acting. When we default to conditional thinking we tend to question, *If ... then ...?* when relating our thoughts to each one another. For instance, *If I give feedback to Sienna, she may react how she did last time.* Straight away, we have referenced what would or could happen in relation to what happened in the past. This is nothing but an assumption; there is no evidence to support how Sienna will respond to the feedback. We naturally relate new thoughts to the old thoughts and then make them mean something. Again, beliefs are things we consider to be true, so like our thoughts these may not always be accurate.

I work with individuals and teams on marketing and presenting their message to large groups both internally and externally. It's amazing to witness and see firsthand how people grow as speakers once they let go of doubt, negative thoughts and self-talk. When they make this new thinking habit a focus, their results, level of confidence and audience engagement sky-rockets.

Our beliefs are powerful. Many years ago, I read a story about an elephant, let's call her Narinda. Like monkeys and bears, Narinda could recognise her own reflection. Highly intelligent and emotional, elephants can mourn the death of another elephant for up to thirty years. As a calf, Narinda was chained to a fence. She was small and weighed only 250 kilograms. Handlers came up with an idea to 'program' elephant calves by self-imposing limiting beliefs into their thinking. When Narinda was first restrained, she tried to escape. She dragged the fence with her as she whined and tugged at the chain. After only a few weeks, she surrendered and stayed chained to the fence for years on end, under the scolding sun and harsh conditions. She had accepted the **fact** that the chain had limited her. With that belief imprinted, she could then be tied with a small rope. As an adult and weighing 8,000 kilograms, she could have easily escaped on such a small rope, but she had wired her thinking that it was impossible. She never attempted to break free because she **knew** she had no chance at all. In Narinda's case, her belief became so strong she couldn't shake it or separate it from reality. Don't succumb to limiting beliefs. Challenge and change up your beliefs to serve and empower you.

Many people struggle with finding true self-belief. They aren't aware of the limiting beliefs that are creating restricting inner boundaries. These keep us stuck. They are not real and are only in our minds. Like an iceberg, we are conscious of the beliefs above the surface—the tip of the iceberg—while the majority remain under the surface at an unconscious level. It's important to remember that the subconscious mind holds the most power over us. To change any limiting beliefs, we firstly need to become aware of them, which is a challenge in itself as these sit at a subconscious level.

So let's look at moving forward. This is great opportunity to look at what you believe in and why it is or isn't working for you. What do you need to change, adapt or let go of? What can you let in or let be?

Awareness

You need to become aware of what needs to change. What are you telling yourself that could be limiting you fulfilling your purpose?

This exercise is a bit like walking into a dark room with a lit candle.

Jot down two limiting beliefs you may have that are affecting your leadership or belief in your ability to execute on plans, purpose or goals.

| Limiting belief 1: | |
| Limiting belief 2: | |

Flip these to be empowering beliefs that will serve you moving forward.

| Empowering belief 1: | |
| Empowering belief 2: | |

By flipping limiting beliefs, you can focus on what you do want and dismiss what you don't want. A constant reminder of these empowering beliefs will assist your mind to sort and perceive the world to make it a reality. This is a great exercise to tap into every now and again to ensure those *dark beliefs* are lit up, changed and lived with purpose.

Remember, don't act like an elephant.

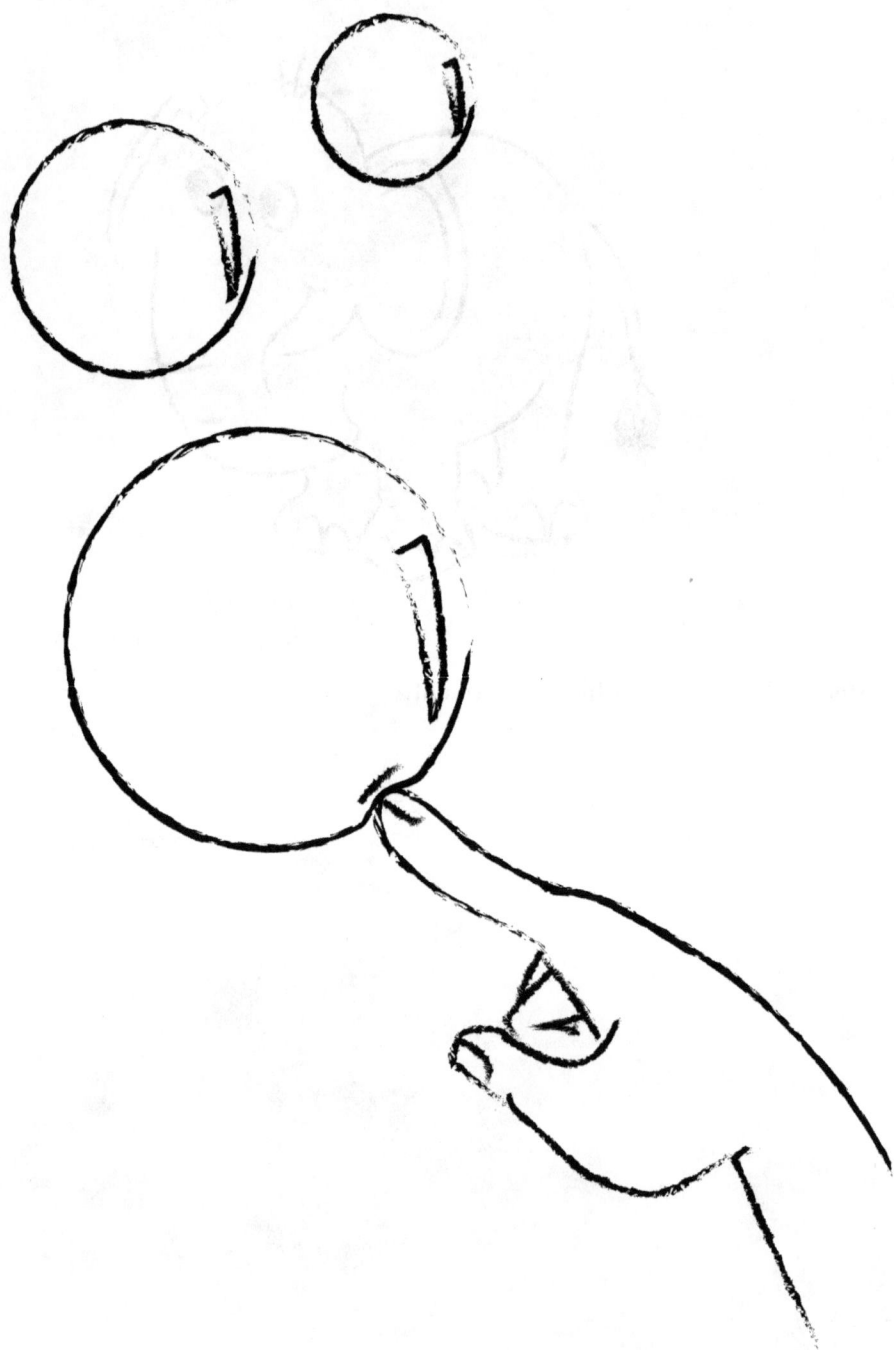

PART FOUR

MINDSET TO
MIND-SHIFT

'The mind is everything. What you think you become.'
—Gautama Buddha

A snow skier embarking on a snowboarding lesson realises that the end goal is the same: both ways will get them down the slope. You can use transferable skills and be ready to attempt something new but at the same time, you have to clear your mind and be open to new ways of thinking when applying this to a new skill. I know this firsthand. I struggled when I attempted to convert from skiing to snowboarding and in no time went back to skiing, as this was my preferred default of getting down the powdery slopes at Hotham. Maybe I gave up due to lack of time to practise a new skill, but it awakened a realisation in me that we can become so hard-wired in doing something one way we forget to question what we do and fail to look at new ways. Mindset can sometimes be underestimated. A strong mindset has kept me going when my sister became ill. I adopted a stronger and more empowering mindset to deal with the situation. I wanted to be the best I could be for her. In turn, her mindset has always been fiercely strong, so mirroring this has served us both well.

Your mindset is like a muscle; it can be trained, strengthened and built to what you want it to be. The key is to question how you do things. This shakes up your day-to-day thinking and has an impact on your actions. With a clear purpose and solid belief in yourself and others, you can develop and nurture a leadership mindset or *mind-shift*. Nothing should be *set*, a shift is fluid and open to change and further development. Effective leaders don't look at things in the same way during their career. What goes on in their head has to change and evolve—much like our beliefs. One mindset won't fuel and serve you forever. Like a tradesman's tool that needs to be serviced and updated in order to perform its specific job. Be open and ready to explore your current mindset around your leadership vision and intent.

Be prepared to update what isn't working. Let in new thoughts, ideas and exercises to build your mindset muscle.

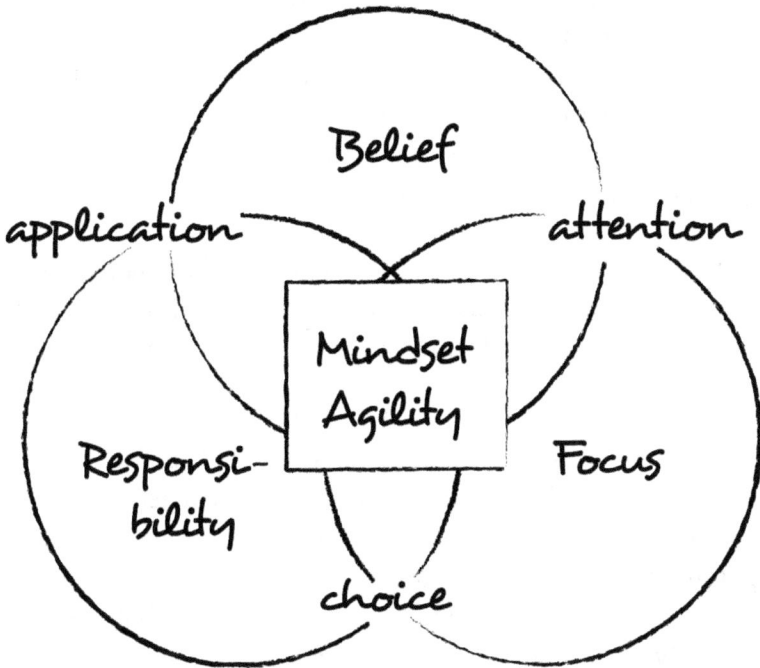

Figure 10: Mindset to Mind Shift

A BUBBLE OR BURSTING MINDSET

'The world as we have created it is a process of our thinking.
It cannot be changed without changing our thinking.'
—Albert Einstein

In life, not just on a professional front, it is imperative to master a strong and disciplined mindset. It can be developed and nurtured over time and will give you the ability and agility to own your thoughts. Your thoughts and way of thinking determine how you feel and enforce the action you do or don't take.

In a leadership role, if you are focusing and building your thoughts on catching your team out, then I can guarantee you will. The mind is an amazing machine and will actually sort and perceive the world to tune in on what you are focusing on. Alternatively, if you believe, as I do, in building a strength-based team, you will identify strengths in all team members and leverage this for the good.

Mindsets are beliefs about you—your talents, intellect, skills. Mindsets reflect who you are. After many years of working with individuals on building and reframing their mindsets, I believe we can adopt one of two defining mindsets.

A Bubble Mindset is simply where you apply the belief that what you have and who you are is set in stone and can't be changed. You are born this way and that's the end of the story. You see yourself, your skills and your potential encapsulated within a bubble. Put simply, you believe they cannot be developed. Individuals living with the bubble mindset give up easily and avoid anything that challenges them. They believe that trying new things is a waste of time. They are not open to feedback, self-growth and development. People living with a bubble mindset feel threatened by the success of others and as a leader may not provide feedback or development to others as they don't believe in it themselves. Overall, this mindset keeps them frozen in time.

We all come across people with this mindset and if, like me, being the polar opposite, you can find it frustrating and toxic. Individuals with this mindset are easy to recognise. In your team, they may be that person who is not coachable, teachable or interested in growing.

A bubble mindset can stem from a fear of something new, aversion to change, rejection, or that their surroundings—role models, culture of their organisation—have wired them that way. If you have a bubble mindset, consider that being half way through this book means your mindset is open to change. I'm often asked if people with a bubble mindset can change. I think they can, depending on the context, their surroundings and their want for change.

Then there is the bursting mindset. When you adopt this mindset, the sky is the limit. This is where you believe intellect can be increased and developed. You take feedback on board and apply it to better yourself. Chances are you like delivering feedback because you believe in it. You believe in the effort to grow yourself and make a continued effort to do this. It is vital that successful leaders have a bursting mindset. Only then can you instil belief in your team and its abilities, and your overall connection with your team and team's results.

With this mindset, you enjoy seeing others succeed. Others may even find you inspiring. I definitely have this type of mindset with growth listed in the top five things I value in my life and work. I naturally gravitate towards people with a bursting mindset who like to learn, unlearn, learn again, evolve, and change. Fostering this mindset ensures you are ready for change—like a dam, your floodgates are open to new tides and ways of doing things.It makes sense to nurture and develop a growth mindset. A bursting mindset can foster motivation and productivity, especially in a leadership role. It also contributes to one of the most important aspects of leadership, which is developing and enhancing relationships.

It makes sense to nurture and develop a growth mindset. A bursting mindset can foster motivation and productivity, especially in a leadership role. It also contributes to one of the most important aspects of leadership, which is developing and enhancing relationships. Use this exercise to reflect on where your mindset focus is:

What mindset occupies your thinking the majority of the time? Bubble or bursting?	
What do you need to let go of or let in to develop further a bursting mindset?	
How can you instil a bursting mindset into those in your team?	
What are your beliefs around being open to growth?	

THE VOICE VS. THE NOISE

'What we think about when we are free to think about
what we will – that is what we are or will soon become.'
—A.W. Tozer

Intent, purpose and self-belief may be in place, but something else can get in the way of a leader's success—I call it 'the noise'. It's the thick, static noise, like a dark cloud ruining a perfect clear blue sky or the white noise annoyingly projecting from a radio that's out of range.

How many times are you side-tracked, disrupted or focused on the noise. It may begin as a wispy white cloud but as you give it more airplay and focus, it grows and becomes darker, thicker and louder.

As a leader the noise doesn't serve you, it subtracts from you and takes you away from the clearly defined and articulated 'voice'. It dilutes the voice—the clearer message you should be taking on board. We all have inner dialogue, yes even you; that voice in your head. I want you to separate the two. Imagine the voice is white; it can serve you well. The noise is dark grey; it is static and does nothing but dilute your intentions. The voice provides clarity while the noise is muffled, uncertain and downright confusing.

Learning to distinguish between the two can be challenging as the noise can assist in self-sabotage and procrastination.

Often we aren't aware of what the noise is or the consequences from letting it guide us. One of my first client coaching sessions was on the phone, and my client kept saying, *they wanted resolution on what sport to play*. Now remember, I'd just left a fantastic career to pursue my own practice and as I paced up and down my office, I was seriously having second thoughts about my newly chosen career path. How could someone be paying me to find out what sport they wanted to play? Surely there were bigger fish to fry or eat.

I removed my thoughts from the picture and focused back on the client. After asking a few powerful questions and embracing uncertainty—and ignoring the noise in my head—together we unwrapped the layers. After ten minutes of silence, my client had a breakthrough. He realised he had been procrastinating in every area of his life including work, moving forward with his spouse, and yes, even choosing a new sport. He couldn't move forward with *the noise* in his head resulting in the thickest procrastination blockage I have ever witnessed. I learnt that in order to serve my clients and use my full potential, I needed to cancel my conversation with the noise—tap in, identify the noise and block it out. I have used the analogy of the Voice Vs. the Noise for many years, and it's a great way to separate the two.

There is a saying, *Only after confusion can there be clarity*, but don't stay confused for too long, clear the heavy fog—the noise—and let the sun shine in.

Learning to differentiate the two is imperative and the key is to keep your mind focused by having clarity in your outputs, energy and the message you are conveying. We all know that feeling of tossing and turning late at night, worrying about something, only to get up in the morning light and realise our restlessness was caused by something trivial. This is because, late at night, confined to our bed in darkness there is nothing we can do to change the throughs that disturb us and, therefore, they are amplified and blown out of proportion.

This model clearly shows where you may be sitting as far as your mindset goes, right now.

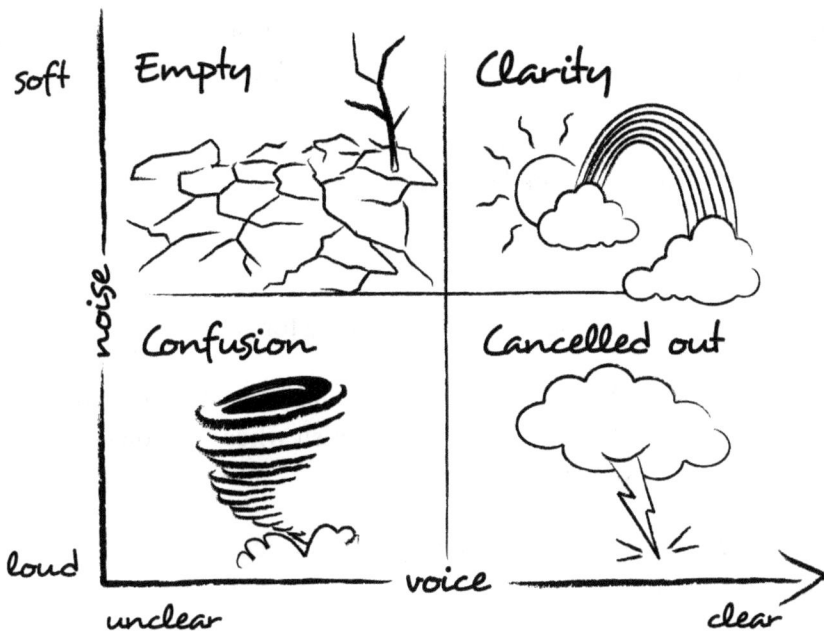

Figure 11: Voice vs. Noise

The clearer the voice and the softer the noise, the more fulfilling your mindset will be. Focus on the voice that serves you as a leader and don't give the noise any airtime. Remember that where your attention goes, your energy flows. Stop having conversations with the noise. Listen to and strengthen the voice.

Here are three tips to get you there.

Awareness

Stop! Yes, you, stop! Sit alone and reflect on what is really going on for you. As a leader of people, self or a leader of conversation and influence: what is driving your mindset?

Mindset can come from your intuition, or your enteric nervous system—let's call it your gut brain. Did you know this brain has as many neurons as a cat and can influence your mood and wellbeing. It is referred to as your second brain. It is tied to commitment, belief and purpose.

mBraining explains further the primal connection between our brain and our gut. Hence, *I have a gut feeling about this* (Soosalu & Oka).

Some of the thoughts that have derived from a deep sinking feeling in your stomach are associated with the noise.

Evidence

Is the inner dialogue you are having working for you?

Can you think of a time, even right now, when that confusing unadulterated noise was at play? Distinguish when the voice is at play and when the noise is creeping in.

Can you think of a time you listened to your voice and the outcome led to a successful result?

Monitor what your gut is telling you as a response to the thoughts you have. I have many clients who keep a journal of this as a way to track patterns and predict when the noise will hit. External factors, like certain people in your life, can contribute to the noise *and* the voice.

Action

Simple, yes. Easy, no. Awareness is the majority of this journey. In short, stop having a conversation with the noise. Do not give it exposure. Do not flip the noise into a positive, as this will only get you more focused on it. Instead, tell it to *nick off* and get into massive action around what the voice you believe in is telling you.

Watch your results from the outside in, and check in to stay on track. Creating a mind-shift that works for you will be a work in progress— this won't happen in a day.

The house you bought before you had children is no longer big enough. Like your mind, change it to serve where you are going. Distinguish the dark and light and see what changes and evolves for you, your team and your organisation.

TREAT MINDSET AS A FEELING, NOT A FACT

'You are what you do, not what you say you'll do.'

—C. G. Jung

Language is such a fascinating thing. Words can change our thoughts and, therefore, our feelings and actions. There is so much focus on the importance of body language and non-verbals that the magic of words can sometimes be lost. They might not account for the majority of our message when face-to-face with others, but when we look at words in the context of our inner dialogue we must not underestimate their power.

Mindset (or mind-shift,) is not a fact. It is not fixed and factual. It is a feeling, a fluid process that can change. For the visuals out there, if mindset were a fact it would look like a solid piece of wood. However, if we consider mindset to be a feeling, it would be like a cascading waterfall—fluid, moving and forever changing as it carves its way through rocks and valleys. Whatever you visualise, my point is that if you consider mindset as a transient process—a feeling—you can be more open to the possibility of it growing and changing. For example, I have always had a passion for writing. From a very young age, I have known I was destined to write a few books. Even in Grade 4, I wrote mini books and poetry. I loved contributing to the school newsletter. As much as I knew I had a book in me—so to speak— due to time constraints and other priorities, it became challenging to find the time. I buried my dream until later in life when I could sit on the beach and write for hours, like in the movies, with my undisturbed ocean view, where I would flush out a book (preferably in daylight with intermittent walks along the beach). At the time, this was not a reality for me. Instead, I have written this book, out of hours, in libraries, cafes, in my car at the side of the road and on weekends and early mornings where I normally would have been socialising, cooking, doing yoga or traipsing around markets and food stores. I made the choice to put all that on hold and make this happen. I viewed the process as an opportunity and a gift, not a challenge. Being challenged is not a fact, being challenged is being homeless or dealing with an incurable illness. In my example, being challenged was simply a feeling made up of uncertainty and hazy priorities where I looked at writing as an indulgent passion instead of a gift that could be part of me, not a separate thing to indulge in if I had the time.

Is it challenging to change your leader mindset? Many clients fight with the *manager* vs. *leader* mindset. Let go of it and look at adopting a leadership mindset as a process. Reflect on the following questions and jot down your answers.

If mindset is not a fact and we consider it a feeling or a process, what do you need to change to open your thinking when next approaching a challenge?	
What needs to change for this mindset to serve you, your team and your organisation?	

> What does a leadership mindset look like for you, right now?

Many of my clients refer to my simple model below. Anything that comes up for you will usually enter your mind, as what you believe to be factual. You can only change this to be a feeling if you take a new perspective by crossing the two ideas of fact and feeling.

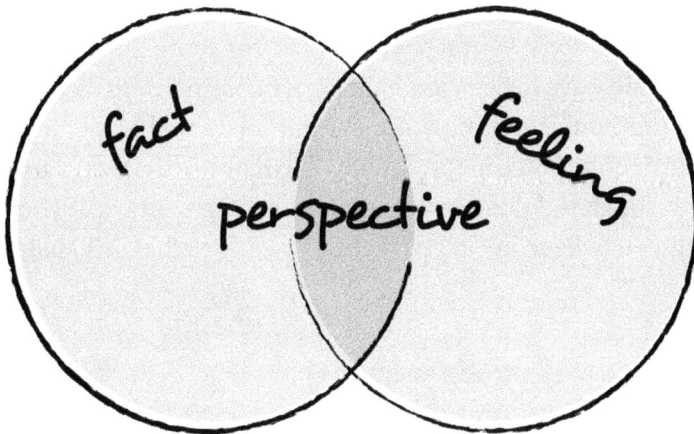

Figure 12: Mindset is a process

YOUR ENERGY IS A MIRROR OF YOUR MINDSET

'A professional is one who does his best work
when he feels the least like working.'
— Frank Lloyd Wright

In the last few chapters, we have worked through identifying your purpose as a leader and building belief in this and yourself. The mindset you adopt, foster and nourish will either assist you to flourish or expire as a leader. You choose your thoughts. Your creed, gender, age, intellect or experience doesn't matter; we all have one thing in common—the choice of thought. Your mind is your own. Yes, it can be tainted or lifted by others but you have to own it and accept you have total freedom of what you think is true, false, hindering or empowering, especially when leading others with your purpose, direction and energy. Energy is shown through your actions. Ultimately, it comes from your mindset. If you run a meeting and have little or no belief in or commitment to the message you are communicating, how do you think you will be perceived? You can't fake energy. You can try, but it will become exhausting and people will see through it. When you do things incongruent with who you are and what you believe in, you play the game of conflict. It's an ugly game to play.

Your actions reflect your mindset

Every action has a thought and feeling attached to it. By simply reading that last sentence, you will have produced an action or thought. Maybe you frowned, maybe you had an answer and maybe you went blank. These thoughts and feelings trigger the actions or behaviours you demonstrate to your team and yourself.

Agility is a mindset, not a process. To adapt and upgrade to agile thinking you need to be able to 'renew your mind'. To get to a point where you doubt things and where you openly say, "I don't know", can assist you in developing yourself and the team you are leading. Having a clear mindset, one that is open to change and new ways of thinking and doing, will serve the greater good.

There are a few things you can focus on:

Responsibility: This is the ability to respond and be fully accountable for all outcomes. This means you need to be 'at cause' and decide— no matter the circumstances—that you will be accountable and take responsibility for the outcomes. Making the choice to self-lead and take responsibility can be a real game changer.

Focus: The old adage, *what you choose to focus on, you will find,* rings true here. Think about an unusual baby's name: until you heard it, it wasn't in your focus or sphere of thought on a subconscious level— now it pops up everywhere. What do you want *from* your team and *for* your team? If you look for issues, you will find them; if you look for competency and have a strengths-focus, you will also find this.

Perspective: Use perspective when faced with limited options that may be preventing you to move forward. An agile leader likes exploring unknown territory, like standing at a cliff face; they aren't led towards certainty. They prefer clarity over certainty and have a clear sense of what is next in order to achieve their overall mission and purpose.

Mindset: This is about being able to discipline your imagination. When you get to a place of, *I don't know,* you are perfectly placed to install upgraded software in your mindset—a new way of thinking. This takes you to a place of curiosity. An agile leader will ask themselves, *What if I did know?* This simple reframe can open up your thinking to a world of possibility and new ways.

In a nutshell, the actions and behaviours we currently display come from what we are thinking. Take a moment to reflect on the current results you and your team are experiencing. What you are experiencing right now comes from actions resulting from your mindset and the mindset of your team. You cannot sail a ship if you don't understand the weather patterns and where you are heading on the map.

Your mindset will dictate what you do, and as I mentioned earlier, you need to be a *human being* before a *human doing*. By reading this book, you are making and taking the time to invest in being a *Limitless Leader*. Take time here to reflect on the following questions. Jot down your answers.

What leader or leaders do you admire? What traits could you emulate?	
What thoughts have served you in the past and propelled you forward?	

What thoughts have resulted in unsuccessful action or reactions?	
How are you going to monitor your actions and the response you get?	

Respond, don't react

I work with an organisation whose mantra is *Take Five*. Simply take a five-minute timeout before you respond. In this way, your response will be well-considered and based on logic rather than spontaneous and full of emotion that forms a reaction you may regret.

In some cases, you may not end up responding at all. Where possible, have a face-to-face conversation and use email only as a last resort. Remember to think and respond—not react.

PART FIVE

MOTIVATION

'You can't build a reputation on what you are going to do.'
—Henry Ford

Motivation is a simple and an often underestimated word, and it has fascinated me for over a decade. It is the fuel that lights people up. Many executives are unaware of what motivates them both at in intrinsic and extrinsic level. How many people do you know—this could be you—who are competent at their jobs but are never totally fulfilled, happy or living *on* purpose? It is important not to do only what you are good at but also what you enjoy. There is a big difference here.

While working in corporate organisations, out of numerous roles there was only one role I never really enjoyed (although I was good at it). Thankfully, all my other roles lit me up. I was more productive in these roles as they didn't feel like work. I call the role I didn't enjoy, a gift. I discovered that what didn't make me happy was a valuable insight for my future to ensure I took on only roles and job functions that I enjoy. You know you are doing what you love when you go to bed Sunday night and look forward to the next day. That's how I feel now that I am running my practice, but there are others who experience the 'Sunday-night dread'. You know, that feeling where you don't want the weekend to end, you've had your dinner and you are still looking to fill the rest of the night up so you don't have to face the week that looms ahead.

Did you know that motivation and attitude account for approximately 65 per cent of the predictability of success in a role? As a leader, you need the skill and knowledge, but these wear off if you are not truly motivated. People think they know what motivates them and others, and they simply manage this. What they really need to do is identify real motivation, then feed, and satisfy these motivations. Find them, feed them and flourish. In my practice, I have briefed hundreds of executives on what motivates them using the amazing iWAM profiling tool to map motivation. The iWAM (Inventory of Work, Attitudes and Motivations) tool recognises that we have 48 different motivations at work, and it identifies these in order of preference. (I call them tapas plates—some are prawns and some are jellyfish.) For the sake of this chapter, we will use other tools and exercises to help you map out what motivates you, then build, and drive this motivation.

There are many neurological drivers of human behaviour that work in conjunction with understanding your motivations and attitudes. When I visualise these, I see a person holding a marionette in front of them with all the drivers sitting behind the puppet, resulting in what we see as behaviour and action. Some of these drivers include values, beliefs and your model of the world. We have our own references and see the world based on our own perspectives and experience. We all have knowledge and skills around certain areas and these can be developed, changed and evolved depending on our focus. We also have our own identity, which can change depending on where we are in our journey. Be mindful that we tend to base our beliefs and values on how we see ourselves. If we go from working *in* a team to working *on* a team, we need to view our identity differently as we have essentially evolved from employee to employer. Don't hold on to your old identity. Be mindful that as you grow and change so does your identity, and how you and others see yourself.

Find out what lights you up and revisit this regularly, as it will change for you over the course of your role and career.

As you will see in the model below, we first need to understand what motivates us at a deep level. What fuels us to do what we do every day? Only by having a deep awareness of this can we can delve into and understand what motivates those around us, including internal and external stakeholders, our team and the clients with whom we may interact.

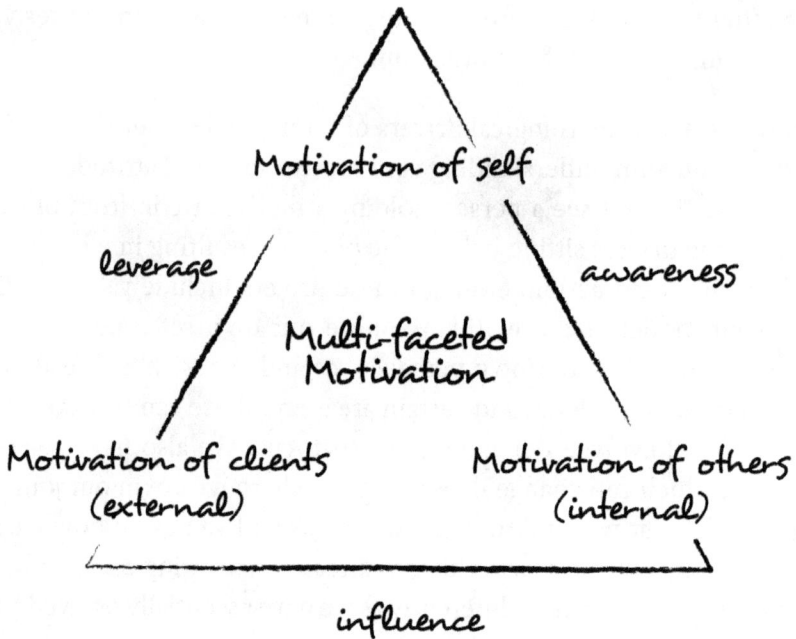

Figure 13: Motivation

MOTIVATION TRUMPS SKILL

'Do you want to know who you are? Don't ask.
Act! Action will delineate and define you.'

—Thomas Jefferson

For decades, motivation has been a major management and leadership issue. It has been the subject of many research studies by figures such as Fredrick Herzberg, Abraham Maslow, John Hunt and Clayton Alderfer. Many of their findings still resonate today but working practises have changed and now there is a focus on variables such as work-life balance, flexible working hours, working virtually (from home) and a shifting focus on performance objectives. We now need to consider motivation from an organisational and individual perspective with a focus, in this chapter, around you, the individual. If you can identify and focus on what motivates and engages you, you can contribute to the motivation and engagement of others at work. Like a lighthouse, to project the blinding light that is emitted out to sea, everything needs to be in order within the lighthouse—a bit like motivation.

During my time as a hands-on leader and working with leaders, I developed the belief that motivation trumps skill. Skill alone is not enough to get us to the top of the mountain. Motivation, either intrinsic or extrinsic, overlays an energy to any skill we master; it's the fuel to succeed and exceed. It's the force behind driving what we know and learn (our skills). Years ago, when recruiting for a large corporate, I interviewed a double degree candidate who ticked all the boxes: IQ, great references and ability to think on his feet. What he didn't emit was the attitude, motivation and energy that all the one-dimensional paperwork had sold him on. He had the knowledge and the skill, but he was missing the will. This was important in such a fast-paced corporate environment and without any evidence of this, the candidate didn't progress to the next level. If you claim to be energetic and driven, at least act it for the interview.

Being deeply self-aware of what motivates you, and those around you, will take your conversations, rapport and sphere of influence to the next level.

To be self-aware you need to be open and committed and take the time to understand what really motivates and energises you at a deeper level.

To do this, you need emotional control and intelligence so you can identify your triggers; leading to building a heightened radar into the triggers of others.

Being self-aware also requires you to get out of what you know—your comfort zone—so you can be open to self-growth and change. We talked about breaking out of your comfort zone earlier, and the importance of this to set the base to be open, ready and aware.

Don't just know and grow your skills. The real gold is tapping into and understanding the depths of what motivates you.

One of the many studies that support my theory was conducted by researchers at the Universities of Munich and Bielefeld, and was published in *Child Development* journal. It suggested motivation and study habits—not intelligence—are the key factors in maths achievement (Paul, 2013).

SELF-MOTIVATION IS ENERGY

'You are energy. What you think begins it. What you feel amplifies it. What you action will determine what happens next.'

—Renée Giarrusso

Tapping into your mind, heart and body from an energetic level can greatly assist self-motivation. When you are in sync with your motivations, you are more aware of how others are motivated.

My brother and sister are people I admire; they both have the ability to stay on track and be motivated in challenging times. Many others would have caved in and given up, but they both have an innate ability to know what they need to do to stay focused and be the best they can be in their current situations. They emit a tenacious energy to keep on going.

In a professional context, being an energetic leader means you can lead and influence a team or decision to high performance, morale and motivation by tapping into the existing motivators, energy, purpose and strength of each individual. By focusing on true commitment, effective communication and authentic connection, you can provide clear direction and motivation to the team, in conjunction with opportunity for individuals, the team and the organisation to grow and succeed. As a leader, your energy can provide the fuel to lead effectively a team and organisation often lacking in direction and will.

Energised people typically choose to behave in ways that enable success. You see them. They stand out and have a contagious aura about them. They are usually proactive, conscientious and resilient. The word resilient comes from the Latin word 'resilire', which means to leap back, or withdraw. It is easier to bounce or leap back if you have deep-seated awareness of what you need in order to do this. Conversely, when people become drained or listless, they are much more likely to act in ways that undermine their success and that of their team. Having a conscious awareness of your motivations will spark your energy because doing what motivates you lights you up from within.

In this model, you can identify where you sit with regard to awareness of your motivation and fulfilling your motivations.

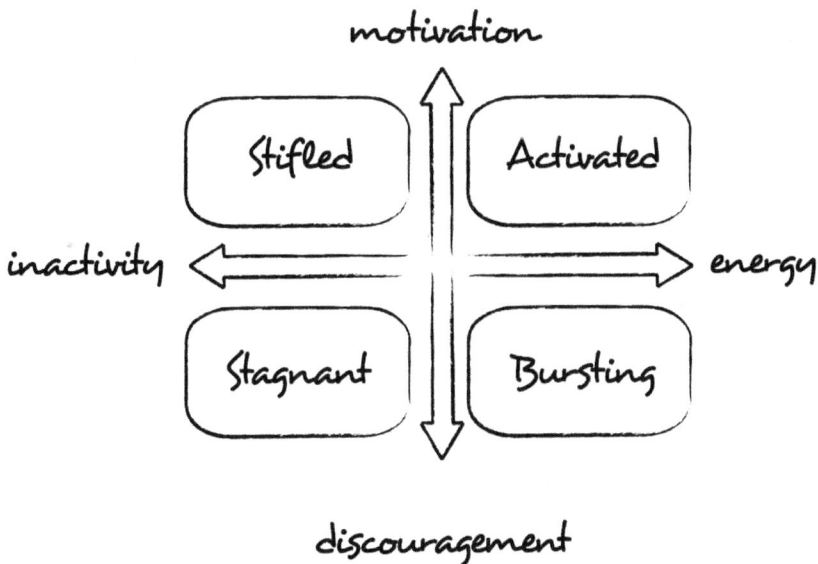

motivation

Stifled	Activated

inactivity ⟵⟶ energy

Stagnant	Bursting

discouragement

Figure 14: Self-Motivation

Stagnant

Here, you are sinking in the mud flats of nowhere. You have low or no motivation, with low activity. Nothing much is happening and you are on autopilot. You do what you do without knowing why. Performance is average here, as you have zero drive. You are plodding along. People in this stage are sometimes labelled lazy; actually, they are usually unaware and bored.

The signs of being in the stagnant quadrant are:

- boredom
- unchallenged
- unawareness of motivation
- low energy and will
- limited activity.

Bursting

At this stage, you are bursting in activity mode. You have no real understanding of what is motivating you but you keep going. I see many people in this quadrant. They are typically running around the office, at all hours, like a tornado, energetically doing a lot of *busy* but not really doing the right things with clear motivational direction. To move up to 'activated' they need to ramp up their awareness of what is really motivating them.

The signs of being in the bursting quadrant are:

- busy
- feeling productive without direction
- scattered
- driven and energetic
- feel like something is missing.

Stifled

In this stage, you are highly motivated but low on energy. This may be due to not getting to do the things that motivate you in your role. This can get tiring, and is often referred to as 'wrong job fit'. We call this stage 'stifled' because here you are a flame continually being snuffed out. To move across to 'activated', you need to have alignment of what motivates you and the role you are doing and then act on it.

The signs of being in the stifled quadrant are:

- low energy
- motivated but no real action
- listless
- incongruent
- unproductive.

The keys to moving to 'activated' are *identifying* and *aligning* what motivates you to your role as a leader, and being disciplined to drive your *awareness* of what is and isn't motivating.

Activated

If you are here, great. This is where you want to be. In 'activated' you are highly motivated and aware of what is driving you. By being authentic to your motivation, there is heart in your energy. Your energy is high, clear and authentic. (We want to capture and bottle the essence of those in this quadrant.) You know what motivates you and you're doing the right things for the right reason. You feel fulfilled and on purpose.

Many leaders in this area cascade this energy onto their teams, which can assist in a high performing team—a *super team*.

The signs of being in the activated quadrant are:

- energetic

- self-aware
- magnetic
- highly motivated
- driven
- in flow.

Self-motivation is internal, and we all have parts of our role that don't motivate us. If we feed and satisfy our motivation at least 70 per cent of the time, we can lead our purpose with real belief and a strong mindset, and project the energy we need to bring our team forward.

Self-motivation can fuel you forward and not only will you gain internal energy; your interpersonal, team and organisational energy will lift. I was once part of a team led by a self-motivated, passionate and driven leader. Their leadership was infectious.

Make no mistake, self-motivation and tapping into this is another layer of the 'being' part of leadership.

> 'Never, never, never give in!'
>
> —Winston S. Churchill

In books to follow, I will cover more on motivation as an integral part of communication. Like a house, this book is the slab, the foundation and the building block for all the 'doing' that lies ahead. Doing this work now will help you project and unleash energy. Remember, you want to match or exceed the frequency of energy you want to create in your team and organisation.

DO WHAT YOU LOVE NOT JUST WHAT YOU ARE GOOD AT

'A ship is safe in harbor, but that's not what ships are for.'
—John A. Shedd

We often think we know what motivates us, especially in a work capacity. Maybe we ended up in a role because we were good at our previous role or we have been there the longest and, therefore, slipped into a new role without much thought as to whether it matched our strengths and what really energises us.

Imagine knowing what really motivates you with a view to then consciously ensuring you satisfy these motivations. Not only will you be happier but you will be in control of your happiness, purpose and achieve fulfilment in your role.

How many people do you know who are great at their roles or successful in their own business but are just not happy? You know ... the person who always says how much they hate their job, the office, the people or, more commonly, their boss. They live for the vacations and public holidays. These people are usually more than competent in their role—this may be you—but no matter the success they enjoy, they are not happy or fulfilled. They are on the treadmill of life, making no choice to change, and becoming victims of their own demise.

A study to test what motivates people from different cultures in a work context found that two key things motivate the majority of people (Pink, Drive: The surprising truth about what motivates us, 2011). These key findings were also expressed and communicated as a powerful RSA animated clip on YouTube. Obviously there are more, but the two key motivators identified were fulfilment and purpose at work. (Based on the thousands of clients with whom I have personally worked, I have to agree with this.) I have witnessed clients in what many people view as successful roles doing their 'purposeful' work outside of their day-to-day job or career.

This is because they are not getting that personal fulfilment and purpose during the week. This has sparked a myriad of charities and philanthropy initiatives outside of the normal working hours, and is a clear indicator that people have a raw need be on purpose and be fulfilled. Two of the six human core needs in life are growth and contribution, and motivation links directly into these.

Money is often perceived as a motivator. I believe the true motivator is more around what money can give you, such as quality of life, time, choice and freedom. You will shine professionally if you are doing what you love, as opposed to what you are good at and don't enjoy. Many senior managers leading large teams tell me they got their role because of the time they had done in their organisation and that they are good with people. To these senior managers, I pose the question, *Do you enjoy leading people?* The response is generally, *Not really, but I am good at it.*

Dianne, is a technically brilliant Regional Manager I mentored over the last two years. She was more than competent in her role. She loved being at the coalface, loved diversity and building relationships. She had a high level of creative and alternative thinking when it came to designing and implementing marketing plans. After a successful 23 months in her role, she was promoted to run a small team of six business managers in a multi-national organisation. She accepted the role as she wanted people management experience and was open to this, as she would also retain ownership of the larger national accounts. Like most people, she jumped in, and after four months realised she was the 'manager who still liked to sell' and found it challenging to differentiate her past role and identity with her new one. She realised the things that drove her were not present in her new people-management role. We worked through what got her out of bed in the morning and how we could align these preferences with the drivers she needed in order to be a successful leader. Two of Dianne's motivators were that she was extremely goal oriented and outcome focused.

She was also a high initiator opposed to a person that would sit back and mull over what should be done. She loved to come up with ideas and get many things moving at once. She was a real self-starter. Nothing could hold her back once she got on that train. She liked to get things done and move on to the next thing. She was a great problem-solver but had an innate desire to pursue and achieve goals and be outcome focused opposed to looking for potential problems and pitfalls. In her new role, she needed to be more of a problem-solver, challenging her team and mentoring them when required. We worked on staying focused on the end goal and using problem-solving as a way to get to that and achieve the outcome. She also learnt to seek out the natural 'problem-solvers' in her team and leverage their energy and strength in this. Dianne is still consciously working on feeding the things that motivate her while linking these to the things that don't. The key here is to identify three things: your skills, your knowledge and your motivations. These three vital things make up competencies that will serve you moving forward.

Brainstorm as many things as you can in column one—the things you are good at. Then circle the things that you *enjoy* and cross out the things you don't. Transfer the things you enjoy (from column one) into column two and add any additional things you enjoy doing in your role.

In my role, what am I good at?	In my role, what do I enjoy?	Motivator

In column three write down the motivator that relates to each thing you enjoy doing at work. An example might be, *Diversity at work is something I enjoy and the motivator for me would be growth.* See below for more ideas of motivations you may have:

Outcome focused	Problem-solver	Making decisions internally	Making decisions with feedback
Doer	Reflector	Creativity	Big picture focus
Detail focus	Team environment	Focus on people	Activity focus
Structure and organising	Conceptual thinking	Teamwork	Individual work
Sole decision-making	Looking to the past	Future thinking	Thinking in the present

Now rate each of your motivators on a scale of 1–5 where 1 is something you never get to do and 5 is something you do all the time.

Choose the lowest three items and ask yourself:

	What specifically can I do to bring more of this preference in?	What do I need to let go of to make space for this?
Item 1:		

Item 2:	
Item 3:	

Revise this exercise every few months. Sometimes we can feel unexplainably flat or slightly off at work when everything is going along fine. This is common, and we usually don't know why we feel like this. This can be a result of our subconscious motivations not being satisfied. You need to be self-motivated. Tapping into your own hot buttons is advantageous not only for you but for your leadership journey and energy.

MOTIVATION IN OVERDRIVE

It's good to be aware that your strengths and the things that motivate you—your energisers—can become your weakness. The things that motivate you, energise you and light you up can also be to your detriment if you overuse them or use them in overdrive. It is similar with strengths; the things you are strong at can sometimes be overused because you are good at them and enjoy doing them. This can occur quite easily, as you may not be aware how often you are doing these things. As they naturally motivate you, you may do them at a subconscious level.

We have both extrinsic and intrinsic motivators. Let's start off by having a look at extrinsic motivation. This type of motivation occurs where the motivational factors are external to us. Our actions here are performed as a means to an end and this is usually valued more than the actual activity itself. An example of this could be exceeding a sales or business target to receive a monetary incentive or an award on stage. Intrinsic motivation is a different case, as the motivating factors emanate from within us and are determined by the way we feel about what we are doing. If working on achieving a business target or incentive, a person may feel they are gaining personal satisfaction, excitement and having fun. These are examples that the person, in this case, is experiencing intrinsic motivation. Intrinsic motivation can have the greatest potential to create an ongoing behaviour of activity and adherence. Social psychologists have long identified that a sense of ownership is crucial for people to feel intrinsically motivated. When an individual experiences development combined with a sense of autonomy over the actual process of development, they will feel an increased boost in their motivation to progress.

Let's have a closer look at motivation in overdrive. One of my key motivators, or the things that energise me, is optimism, which means I am highly motivated by being in a work environment where having a positive outlook and being able to remain optimistic is accepted. I can easily stay positive and outcome focused at the most challenging times. A defining moment that displayed this for me was when I was going for my first real job in a global company in my early twenties. I got through five of six gruelling stages and it was down to myself and one other candidate to present at a final assessment centre at 9 am on a Tuesday morning. I had put hours into my marketing presentation and rehearsed it to the hilt. I had organised a lift from one of my best friends into the city for the Tuesday morning, had practised my presentation and had even lashed out on yet another outfit, all in the hope to secure the job. On the Monday night, I received an unexpected phone call.

I was actually out watching a movie when I got the call from my Mum saying I needed to come home and that something had happened. I will never forget that drive, with my now husband, whom I had only just met. I went into autopilot; I was determined to get home and find out what had happened. I arrived at my Mum and stepdad's house, where I was living at the time. Mum opened the door puffy-eyed and in tears. My whole world stood still in that moment. I was shocked to hear Dad was unwell. He was in hospital. We got back in the car and sped to the hospital and in a blur of uncertainty and tears, we ran into emergency. My Dad, who I was very close to—had just passed away. I was horrified, devastated and overwhelmed with such a sudden loss. Although he had just passed on, I got to hold his hand and say goodbye. It was the most surreal experience of my life. Holding his warm hand that I kissed a million times as the nurse held me up, I said an emotional goodbye with little feeling of closure and comprehension of what just happened. The drive home to my family was in total numbing silence. We were all in shock and we were speechless. There were so many questions. Reality hit me when I remembered I had my assessment the next morning. What was I going to do? Should I go? Should I cancel? I saw my Dad every week. We were close and were similar in many ways. He had been an avid entrepreneur with amazing ideas, dreams and a knack for technology and music. I hadn't seen him for over two weeks, which was rare, and this was because the last thing he said to me was, *Get that job, it will set you up. I know you can get it.* Those words resounded in my mind all night and guess what? I called my friend to let her know what had happened and to confirm she would still need to drive me to the city.

I didn't sleep that night, and with a foggy head and a heavy heart I got ready the following morning, armed with my presentation, a stomach full of butterflies and total uncertainty of how I was going to hold up. The assessment went well. I somehow put all my emotions aside, believed in myself, and focused on getting the role. By the end, I was emotionally drained, physically dizzy and when asked about relocating if I got the role I let the panel know what had happened. I'm not going to say it was easy; it was probably the most challenging thing I have ever done, but I had so much determination and a positive anchor in getting the role that nothing could stop me. I ended up getting the job and spent a decade with what was an amazing and career building company. Some people may call me ruthless, insensitive and crazy; I even questioned myself on this at the time, but my optimism and positive outlook went into overdrive and got me through. This is an example of when the motivation of optimism in overdrive worked for me.

Many years later, this same motivation of 'optimism in overdrive' worked in the reverse when a colleague commented that when we sometimes didn't land certain projects we had pitched, I moved on too easily and maybe didn't look at why we didn't get the work. This opened my eyes to the fact that I needed to look into why some of the work we pitched didn't go through. The lesson here was that at times I needed to be more realistic and lower my positivity. This lesson has served me well in running my practice. I have learnt that it is okay and acceptable to be open and show some vulnerability at times in order to grow, learn and have realistic expectations. When working with people who may have different motivators to ourselves, we need to be conscious of these in order to work even better together and complement each other. In this example my colleague was more of a realist and was motivated to solve problems, where as I was goal oriented and optimistic. This frustrated her as she saw me as unrealistic; whereas I saw her as being negative. In either case, we were both right but just needed to understand each other better and fine-tune the level of what motivated each of us.

I wanted to share my story with you because we need to look at what motivates us at an individual level and dial it up or down accordingly.

Others may see the world differently to you. Feed and satisfy what motivates you, but always check in to ensure your self-motivators aren't in overdrive and to the detriment of you and others around you.

PART SIX

ACCOUNTABILITY VS. OWNERSHIP

'The price of greatness is responsibility.'

—Winston S. Churchill

Many years ago, sports coach and co-founder of Nike, Bill Bowerman, made a statement from a position of some experience, 'If you have a body, you are an athlete'. He made this statement a foundation of the business, Nike, a global success that is still breaking rules today. This statement, despite its vintage, is enough to make us sit up and listen. A statement like this isn't just words, it's a trigger to make you stop and realise your potential, and that every day you can grow and use the time as an opportunity to advance.

Statements like this can spark us to be accountable and take ownership. Ownership comes from the inside; you cannot force it. Owning something means it needs to be aligned with your purpose, values and beliefs. From there, you need to apply a strong mindset and be motivated internally and externally to achieve whatever you set out to do. To me, accountability, to account for one's activities and be responsible for them, is often overlooked and many times confused with the word *ownership*. Accountability is usually assigned, and actions could include giving feedback, coaching team members, delegating and setting the vision of the team and organisation. Ownership is more around possessing, or the state of being an owner.

You may lead a team on a deadline where all involved are accountable for the activities and work to drive this. Each person needs to take ownership of the piece they are looking after. Only they can fulfil this ownership. It's almost like an internal driver. I believe to excel in your leadership, at any level, you need to be accountable, responsible and just as importantly, you need to own it—take ownership from deep inside. Ownership is intrinsic and accountability is extrinsic.

Cerise, was a highly competent senior leader. I worked with her as she led a technically brilliant team. After running a focus group and some client surveys we identified that all individuals could sharpen up on their soft skills. Cerise bought me in to assist in growing this team to be even better communicators with internal and external stakeholders and clients. We collaborated closely on the build of the program and getting the buy-in from the team to ensure it wasn't just a one-off event—one of my pet hates. Two weeks prior to the workshop, Cerise informed me she wouldn't be present during the two-day program. She felt she had contributed enough and her investment on the program was done. I questioned the fact that for her to take full ownership of the program, especially after I was gone, it was imperative for her to be part of the program and to be seen as part of the team and the process. In turn, this would assist in letting her team know that leaders in their business believed in development like this. Cerise was hesitant and after what was quite a powerful and challenging conversation we unlocked that she was afraid the engagement would be low due to an impending restructure and she didn't want to see all of her work go to waste. This belief was holding her back. She could not take full ownership of the project. In the end, Cerise not only attended the workshop, she was an integral part of the hands-on activities. This showed accountability for getting the program up and running and ownership that she truly believed in it. The flow-on effect was amazing, with Cerise running the program internally with my occasional assistance to keep it fresh and evolving.

I once designed and rolled out a program, across four states in a three-week period, working closely with a sales director of an organisation. I tailored the capability program to solve their problems and address immediate needs and opportunities at a business level. The sales director opened every workshop in collaboration with me. I was blown away; this doesn't happen often, and it was a large program. It was a first for this business and he wanted the team to know how serious the company was in investing in and growing their future leaders. He talked through how we had met and worked together on the program and how we came to be here. This showed ownership at the deepest level, and I witnessed it firsthand. With his commitment and interaction at a state level, along with what was a dynamic program delivered in an interactive way, the uptake and engagement was effective, long lasting and runs in-house to this day.

Accountability is what people see and ownership is what people feel. It has an energy about it and I look forward to breaking this down over the next few chapters.

'I have been impressed with the urgency of doing. Knowing is not enough; we must apply. Being willing is not enough; we must do.'
—Leonardo Da Vinci

BREAKING DOWN ACCOUNTABILITY

'Action springs not from thought, but from a readiness for responsibility.'
—Dietrich Bonhoeffer

Accountability has many parts. A bit like ingredients in a recipe, only when combined with true ownership can the cake rise and be a success.

If I think back to my first ever job, I was consciously aware only of self-accountability, being accountable for my own actions. Over the years, I have achieved 'dream diversity', which I love. This made me realise that being accountable to myself is only part of the puzzle. I am accountable to my family, I am accountable to clients and organisations, and I am accountable to those colleagues and contractors who work closely with me. I have to take ownership of all I am accountable for, so I can to do it well and with success.

Separating the parts of the accountability pie can help me see where I am. I view accountability as five separate tapas plates. Each is different and diverse, but together they make up the entire meal.

Figure 15: Tapas Plates of Accountability

Tapas Plate 1: Self

This accountability relates to all the actions I set out to do, like a project for which I have taken sole responsibility. This may be the sell in or design of a workshop that I will facilitate, or a keynote speech I need to create and deliver. For you, it could be the structuring of a team or a conference.

You must book the venue, create the agenda and communicate this to those involved. Or it could be designing a strategy for your team or division.

The responsibility is on you and if full ownership isn't taken on here, it will be challenging to take ownership of the other parts that make up accountability.

- Take individual ownership
- Know, own and exceed your KPIs
- Have tools in place to self-evaluate, monitor and action
- Schedule something to keep your goal alive
- Set yourself 'over and above' goals.

Tapas Plate 2: Others and team

Here we need to be accountable to our team, peers and others with whom we work. When we don't take responsibility this will result in us letting our team or colleagues down. Maybe you are working on a team or business strategy and have formed a project team for this. Everyone is in flow and working together when something grabs your attention and takes up your time—you have to put the project on hold. This will impact the group, the credibility of the project, and trust in you as a leader.

- Be open to peers and your team about what you are working on
- Understand others' roles and responsibilities
- Lean in for support and resource
- Buddy with someone on similar projects/customers
- As a team, work on common goals
- Hold each other accountable.

Tapas Plate 3: Clients/external

We don't all have direct clients, but I ask you, *Who is the consumer of what you do?*

Whether or not you are at the coalface, you have accountability to the end consumer or client. If you work in a food or beverage company this will be cafes, restaurants and the families who eat there. If you are a digital media company, your clients may be medium-to- large multi-nationals and then the clients these companies reach. We all have a widespread footprint of accountability. Make sure you know who constitutes this. For me, I work in over 20 industries at many levels, so my accountability has a ripple effect as all interactions are linked.

Share your plans with clients where applicable. Clients will only know what you tell them

- Involve clients in decisions and help solve their spoken and unspoken problems

- Collaborate with them on achieving success and shared accountability. People own what they co-create

- Make sure accountability between you and them is evenly weighted.

Tapas Plate 4: Organisation or business

Standing for your own values is great, and in an ideal world, these would align nicely with those of where you work. When these values are misaligned it shows that a lack of accountability to the organisation or business where you work puts everything in jeopardy. You are the face of where you work, so lack of accountability to self and your team can result in a bigger lack of accountability to your business.

- Be accountable for the results of the team

- Keep others up to date

- Ask for help when needed

- Advise when slippage may occur

- Go over and above when necessary

- Represent your organisation as part of your personal brand.

Tapas Plate 5: Significant others

There is no sequence or priority to these streams of accountability and this one is just as important as the rest. If you revisit your 'why', I am sure family or a significant other would be part of this. For this reason, make sure you are consciously aware of your accountability to them. Most people strive to be the best they can be, but if this is at the price of family, I ask you, *Is it really worth it?* I work long hours. I love what I do but I need to ensure this does not blur the line of accountability I have to invest in my relationship with my amazing husband and close family and friends.

- Set ecological expectations
- Make sure your goals intertwine. (There is no point aiming for a promotion overseas if your partner is not willing to make the move)
- Revisit your professional and personal 'why'
- Use your family as a supportive resource; let them know what you are doing.

Rate yourself on a scale of 1–5 in each area of accountability in the grid below. (5 is having high accountability and 1 is having low accountability.)

Self	Team and peers	Organisation or business	Clients/ external	Significant others

Next, ask yourself:

What do I need to do to dial each area towards 5?	
How am I going to do this?	
What motivators do I need to dial up OR dial down?	
What are the first two steps, and be specific. Use the SMART or TADD models.	

By when will I achieve this?	
Who or what resources do I need to assist me?	

Now, on a separate piece of paper, create an action plan for each of the five areas of accountability.

CADENCE OF OWNERBILITY

'Far away there in the sunshine are my highest aspirations. I may not reach them, but I can look up and see their beauty, believe in them, and try to follow where they lead.'

—Louisa May Alcott

Accountability and ownership are two different things. When fused together, I call it 'Ownerbility'. It's the ability to take full responsibility and ownership. Accountability is external and is usually the means to an end. Accountability is something that is assigned to you or something you have been asked to do. When this happens, whoever assigned the accountability is still the owner of it—a reason delegation has to be thoroughly considered.

Some of the guiding principles of accountability include:

- How we make a commitment to each other
- How we measure and monitor progress
- How we respond when things don't go as planned
- How much ownership we actually take to get things done
- How we respond when others let us or the team down.

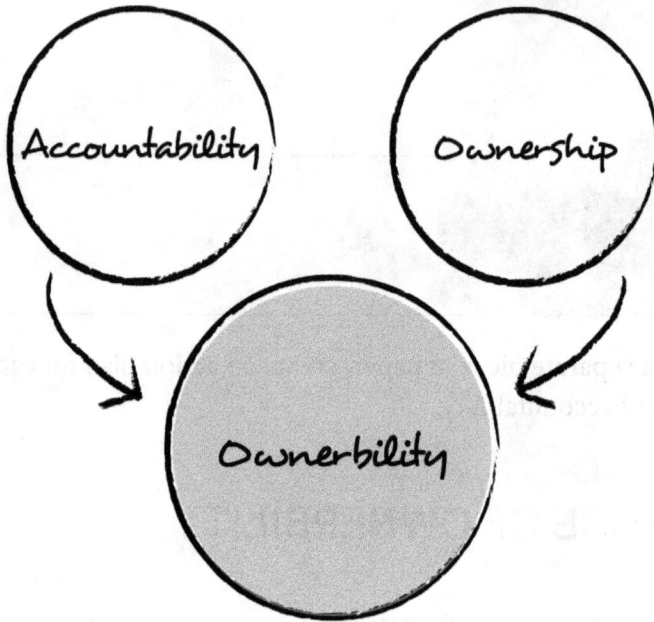

Figure 16: Ownerbility Model

Ownership is more around possessing, or the state of being an owner—taking ownership of something. Ownership cannot be taught, but, as a leader, you can portray ownership that will cascade and, in essence, become part of your team's culture. When compared to accountability, ownership is not given to you or assigned to you; it is, in most cases, taken. When your manager gives you something, he or she cannot assign ownership. In the same way, you cannot assign ownership to those in your team.

The guiding principles of ownership include:

- How we are going to make something happen
- The success measures that can be put in place
- Ensure full internal commitment and attachment to completing
- Embrace a feeling of care and responsibility.

There are many things, right now, in your position for which you need to take ownership. You need to commit internally to saying *I am going to make this happen.*

Let's have a look at your key accountabilities and what ownership you need to take to move forward with them. Place one item of accountability in each shaded area. Simply list key points of accountability you have right now, in your current role. Map down and complete each column in detail. Sometimes it is easier to disassociate in order to come up with answers.

What do I need to do to make this happen?			
What emotions/ beliefs will assist me to achieve this?			
What will I accomplish?			
How will I measure success?			

What would I tell someone else to do to achieve this?	
What would they accomplish if they followed this suggestion?	
What things could I suggest to them to measure this in order to achieve success?	

This exercise is a good way to ensure you take 'Ownerbility' in your leadership. By doing this, you clearly see the 'what' of what you need to do and can attach internal measures to make it happen. This is a great activity to undertake as a one-on-one exercise or as a team to promote buy in and expectations around tasks and responsibilities you may assign, or that are assigned by others. This book is all about you, so I encourage you to do this first and make it part of your thinking and action moving forward.

PLAN TO ACTION

In a study at Dominican University, California, 179 participants were separated into five groups and asked to explore various ways of setting goals. All groups were asked to set goals for a four-week period. Group 1 was asked to *think* about their goals and groups 2–5 were asked to *write* their goals (among other goal-setting tasks). After four weeks, the participants were asked to rate their progress in accomplishing their goals. It was found that the groups with written goals achieved significantly more than the group without written goals (75 per cent from group 5 compared with 43 per cent in group 1). This study concluded that written goals enhance goal achievement, as goals are supported in a positive way (Matthews).

This study is one of many that prove that having a clear vision or written goal can set you on the path to success.

Years ago I mentored a well-known business owner who never believed in setting goals and commented, *Well, I've done pretty well without them,* to which I responded, *Imagine if you had set a focus, maybe you would have done this even easier, more quickly and more effortlessly.*

What you set out to do needs to be personal, ecological and important to you. If you didn't care if someone took away your plan, then it's not one you will most likely pursue. Some of you may have heard of SMART goal setting (Specific, Measurable, Attainable, Relevant, Timely). I think having specific, forward thinking and measurable goals are important, and yes, they need to be achievable and relevant but, for me, making time to complete them trumps all the others steps in SMART goal setting. When we set a date for what we need to do, our mind naturally sorts and perceives the world around us to make this happen. It also makes us accountable.

Many people avoid making plans to reach their outcomes. Here are a few reasons why:

- Fear of rejection

- Fear of failure
- The inability to set up a plan
- Lack of clarity around outcome
- They don't have the time
- They misunderstand what achievement can give them
- Being in a 'bubble' mindset.

What will it cost you not to make a plan and achieve it? What will it cost your leadership and future growth? What won't happen?

I'd like to share a simple acronym for moving towards your plan, TADD. (I named it after Tadd Dameron—a famous American jazz composer, pianist and arranger.) It's easy to remember, and following this structure will assist in building your cadence or rhythm of accountability and ownership.

TAAD

T-Towards

Make a forward or towards thinking statement. Simply state what you do want, not what you don't want.

For example, I coached an executive client, Peter, through a career transition. This is one of our conversations:

"I don't want to work in an office." Said Peter.

"Where *do* you want?" I asked.

"I don't want to work as part of a big team."

"Where would you like to work?"

"I'd like to work outdoors in a sole-type role."

Bingo! When we eliminated what Peter did not want, the space opened to a million opportunities and we were able to establish a path forwards—not backwards, where nothing changes.

A-AIM HIGH

If your plan is a walk in the park with little stress then it's not a game changer. Make sure whatever you choose feels a bit uncomfortable. Remember, all growth, as we mentioned earlier, is outside of your comfort zone. This will drive you forward and propel you to achieve what you need. Tap into your motivations to fuel you and realign your beliefs and mindset to assist you. It helps to have some fun, and do what you enjoy along the way. Achieving the outcome is great but enjoy the journey too. Learn along the way as this is the part you will remember. It will assist you in achieving other goals down the track when the going gets tough.

D-DISSECT

How and when do you plan to stop and check in? Plan when you will monitor and evaluate how far you have come and what you need to do. How will you do this? Set date increments that challenge you and keep you accountable to self and your team. Depending on what you aim to achieve, dissect where you are relevant to the goal and your timeline to achieve this. Sometimes, if we have aimed too high in our goals, we can create *overwhelm* and, therefore, become stifled and not move ahead. If this is the case, we need to break the goal down into mini goals and actions to make the end goal achievable.

D-DATE IT

If you can't put a date on it, what are you doing? Be specific, realistic and relevant to your outcome. A date will provide subconscious increments of time for you to achieve whatever you set out to do. I know firsthand how powerful this has been for me in achieving what I have. When writing this book I had a date to get the final copy to my editor; I set a date that would challenge me, but also drive me. I broke this down to how many words per day I needed to write to reach my goal date.

Let's have a look at five key things you can do to bring *Limitless Leadership* into your role. Remember, you don't have to be leading a team; it could be a focus on your self-leadership or a plan around how you will lead and influence a crucial decision or change in the team or organisation you work with or for.

Reflect on the top 5 key objectives you would like to bring to life as a result of investing in the time to read this book. Make sure each one passes the TADD test.

1.

2.

3.

| 4. | |
| 5. | |

Make sure that you check in and that your plan for applying this book is congruent and relevant as to where you are and where you want to go.

Monitor, review and evaluate, and never stop being a *Limitless Leader*.

AFTERWORD

MAKE IT HAPPEN

'You always have two choices: your commitment versus your fear.'
—Sammy Davis Jr.

For me, being limitless is about making the choice to go beyond what I currently know and do and to be the best version of myself. Being limitless, in any sense, is a never- ending journey with healthy dissatisfaction to grow, contribute and be everything we have within us. We all have the choice to create and break the boundaries we set, and only through this is our true potential realised and shared with those to whom we contribute.

My deepest thank you goes to you, the reader, for taking the time to read this book. My wish for you is that my stories, thoughts and words have resonated with you and given you an opportunity to stop and reflect on what this means for you, now and in your future.

With a clear purpose in place, an unwavering self-belief and a 'can do' mindset, you are now in a position to tap into your motivation to get there.

Setting goals to bring your plan to life helps keep them at the forefront, and as a focus. You get what you focus on to the exclusion of all else. Think of a magnifying glass skimming over a patch of dry leaves; if you keep moving it, none of the leaves will catch fire. Stop and focus the beam on one leaf and it will come alight.

With so much going on, it's easy to dilute your focus and do a lot of things well, but none to the fruition and intensity that they deserve.

Never stop learning, never stop growing and share your insights to spread the ripple of being a *Limitless Leader*.

WORKS CITED

Branson, R. (2016). Retrieved from Virgin Unite: https://www.virgin.com/unite/

Burkeman, O. (2013, November 9). This column will change your life: do you feel a fraud? *The Guardian*. Retrieved July 9, 2017, from https://www.theguardian.com/lifeandstyle/2013/nov/09/impostor-syndrome-oliver-burkeman

Cambridge University Press. (2016). Retrieved July 17, 2016, from Cambridge Dictionary: http://dictionary.cambridge.org/dictionary/english/commitment

Craig, N., & Scott A, S. (2014, May). From purpose to impact. *Harvard Business Review*. Retrieved July 19, 2016, from https://hbr.org/2014/05/from-purpose-to-impact

Fox, D. J. (2015). *How to lead a quest: A handbook for pioneering executives*. Wiley.

Goldberg, D. A. (n.d.). *Self-Confidence*. Retrieved 2016, from Competitive Advantage: Peak performance and overcoming sports fears and blocks: https://www.competitivedge.com/self-confidence

Google Company. (n.d.). *Google*. Retrieved from https://www.google.com/about/company/

Horowitz, A. (2011, April 26). *15 people who were fired before they became filthy rich*. Retrieved from Business Insider Australia: http://www.businessinsider.com.au/15-people-who-were-fired-before-they-became-filthy-rich-2011-4?r=US&IR=T#walt-disneys-newspaper-editor-told-the-aspiring-cartoonist-he-wasnt-creative-enough-1

Matthews, D. G. (n.d.). *Study focuses on strategies for achieving goals, resolutions.* Retrieved from Dominican University of California: http://www.dominican.edu/dominicannews/study-highlights-strategies-for-achieving-goals

Mission Statement. (2009, June 2). Retrieved from The Economist: http://www.economist.com/node/13766375

Moss, D. S. (2009). Retrieved from Psychlopedia: Everything Psychology: http://www.psych-it.com.au/psychlopedia/author.asp?author=smoss2

Paul, A. M. (2013, January 3). *Motivation and study habits trump intelligence when learning.* Retrieved from Business Insider Australia: http://www.businessinsider.com.au/how-to-improve-math-skills-2013-1

Pink, D. H. (2010). Retrieved from YouTube: https://www.youtube.com/watch?v=u6XAPnuFjJc

Pink, D. H. (2011). *Drive: The surprising truth about what motivates us.* Riverhead Books.

Rooke, D., & Torbert, W. (2005, April). *Seven transformations of leadership.* Retrieved July 17, 2016, from Harvard Business Review: https://hbr.org/2005/04/seven-transformations-of-leadership

Soosalu, G., & Oka, M. (n.d.). *mBraining: Using your multiple brains to do cool stuff* (Kindle ed.).

Turock, A. (2015). Retrieved from Art Turock's Leadership Development: http://www.turock.com/

MORE ABOUT RENÉE

Renée is obsessed with seeing people reach their full potential. She passionately works with leaders and their teams to achieve this and flourish. She ensures leaders walk away equipped with key enablers and tools to guarantee success and feel even more confidence, motivation and connection to their teams and their leadership brand. Her expertise lies in growing and developing individuals, teams and organisations in leadership, communication and sales capability. She also works on mapping motivation for success and collaboration in teams.

For over nine years, she has been successful in maximising the potential of individuals and teams to excel to the next level. Her 15 years' hands on experience in senior leadership and sales roles gives her credibility and a deep understanding of what it takes to lead a high performing collaborative team and business to success status.

Renée works with individuals and organisations who want to better themselves and to date has attracted hundreds of clients from over 24 industries. These include industries such as FMCG, telco, automotive, consumer durables, government (job services), not-for-profit, electronics, engineering, real estate and professional services.

Renée is aware of the day-to-day workplace pressures and challenges to perform in today's corporate business environment. Those with whom Renée has worked appreciate her dynamic flair, energy and passion to assist others to grow and achieve even more success. With an appetite for life and learning, she is continually enjoying the rewards of running a practice and contributing to the growth and potential of others.

Renée is a keynote speaker, Accredited Associate Coach (ACC), professional trainer and facilitator who works with individuals and teams to unlock inner potential to maximise and realise strengths and capability back on the job.

Renée gains a great level of personal fulfilment from working with a range of clients to realise the transformational benefits that tailored development can provide at an individual and team level. With a focus on leadership, communication and sales effectiveness, Renée has worked with hundreds of clients and industries: GS1 Australia, Snack Brands Australia, Australia Post, George Weston Foods (Tip Top and Don KRC), Mazda, Cookers Bulk Oils, Callaway Golf, Intrax Engineering, Impos, William Adams and many more.

WORK WITH RENÉE

Renée tailors leadership, communication and sales capability programs to match clients' needs by understanding the problems they need solved and working with them to collaborate on the success of embedding these learnings back in the workplace.

If you are looking for an inspirational and dynamic speaker for your next event, engage Renée. You are promised a session that will inform and inspire. Renée specialises in communication, mapping motivation and leadership and will tailor the session to your objectives, audience and timeframe. Sessions are as a keynote presentation or as an interactive workshop. Bringing in an external speaker can effectively lift engagement, and add variety and another perspective to your event

Her *Limitless Leadership* workshop program was born out of her 18 years' experience at the coalface of leadership. It is designed to three leadership levels and is run in-house. The program consists of three different two-day workshops run across 18 months with coaching immersions in between for individual attendees. The overarching objective of the program is to transition from a management mindset to a leadership mindset—a fantastic pathway for future leaders, emerging leaders and senior leadership teams. She also runs a two-day intense Limitless Leadership public program around Australia.

The Top Fifteen Percent Leader is a program run by Renée and her colleague Rohan Dredge, where over a one-year period, they run an openly facilitated mentoring session to the same group of leaders within a business. This takes place as monthly immersions working on real life scenarios, in real time, as a group. This program is highly interactive and dynamic, and it is where the subjective challenges of leadership are addressed so leaders can become less time poor and skill stretched, and more focused on being co-creative and strategic.

Visit http://thetopfifteenpercentleader.com.au for more details.

Mapping Motivation for Success is a workshop that helps teams identify personal drivers and motivators at work, and ways to complement others within the team in order to maximise effectiveness and collaboration.

The workshop helps to motivate the team and create a better understanding of each other's strengths and the utilisation of those strengths to get the best out of each other. It also delves into ways to decode language to understand what motivates others, including external stakeholders.

The iWAM tool is used within this one-day workshop to map motivations of individuals and the team. iWAM is also a hiring tool and can assist in building models of strong performers against which to recruit.

Renée finds running her practice extremely rewarding and has proven results in assisting clients to lead a more empowering life on both professional and personal levels. Her bubbly personality and desire to develop and grow her clients has her working across a broad array of industries and organisations.

For more details, visit www.reneegiarrusso.com or connect with Renée on the following links:

Facebook: ReneeGiarrussoConsulting

LinkedIn: au.linkedin.com/in/reneegiarrusso

Twitter: @Renee_Giarrusso

WHAT CLIENTS ARE SAYING

It's rare that you come across standout talent like Renée. I was in awe of Renée's ability to command a room and get people on board with ideas on easy-to-use coaching and leadership models. Her energy and passion was so inspiring and engaging. "Talk about motivating". As a trainer, coach, mentor, leader and facilitator, Renée earns my highest recommendation.'

>>

'Renée's character, passion and delivery need to be bottled and sent to every business and organisation. The skills provided and constructive feedback has empowered an entire team in just three days.'

>>

'Renée delivers on her promise of helping leaders and teams achieve their potential. Her guidance, coaching and mentoring over the past two years have helped me build a successful team that has achieved growth in excess of 100%.'

>>

'Renée was amazing, great knowledge and brilliant presentation, I learnt so much!'

>>

'I would highly recommend Renée's leadership and communication programs to any middle or senior leaders. It is for anyone who wants to refresh and grow their leadership skills. This workshop has given me the practical skill and knowledge to strengthen my skills as a leader. Renée's experience, insights and coaching experience were brilliant!'

»

'Renée!!! She was fabulous and brilliant with her training! Loved every bit of the program, which offered so much value and insight!'

»

'Renée has assisted us with a range of coaching and communication tools together with easy to implement methodology. Renée is a specialist in iWAM, a job EQ assessment program. We ran this assessment across our management team, which delivered strong insights into workplace behaviour and communication needs. In 2012, Renée designed a two-day 'Developing Managers' workshop from scratch. This piece of work is so well written; it has fully met our needs for developing new and existing managers to achieve even greater performance from their teams. I recommend Renée Giarrusso to any company looking for an outstanding provider who can deliver tailored consulting and training solutions that make a difference at both the commercial and personal levels. They are worthy of consideration for any short list.'

»

'I highly recommend Renée as an executive coach. I found her knowledge and expertise helped me enormously. Renée's extensive FMCG sales experience and great interpersonal skills made the process easy, but it's her extensive knowledge of current coaching tools including iWAM that got me a far better understanding of my motivators and goals, fast results and a great new job within days of my last session.'

»

'We have engaged Renée in facilitating all of our frontline sales training programs. She not only facilitated but also was heavily involved in the development of the material and ensuring it was relevant and engaging for the participants. Renée worked closely with a field representative in each state to ensure the material had our DNA throughout and that she had a thorough understanding of the way we operate, our challenges and our opportunities. Renée has a depth of experience from many sales roles that she draws on during the sessions and that bring a heightened sense of reality to the program. It's not just someone preaching the theory, Renée is someone who has learned from experience and enjoys sharing that experience with others.'

»

'Renée is a confident, professional and effective coach/trainer. I had the privilege to attend one of her sessions and found it refreshing. She knows her subject field and is very good in involving people in her discussions. Her coaching ability for managers is practical and easy to follow. I applied a few of her influencing ideas and had immediate success. One of Renée's specialties is to identify skill barriers and offer practical ways to overcome them. Renée is a confident speaker who will captivate any crowd she addresses. I've also found her website helpful and easy to navigate.'

»

'Renée is a gifted management consultant with extensive experience in training, facilitation and executive coaching. She knows a variety of creative teaching methods to ensure you learn what you need to. Her calming and confident personality makes you feel comfortable and remain engaged during her sessions. Renée is excellent at encouraging trainees to have a go at difficult circumstances. She has an infectious great attitude. Renée is the best trainer I have ever had, there is no price worth her training sessions if you want to be a great manager and leader.'

»

'Renée is very well organised, efficient, extremely competent, and has an excellent rapport with people of all ages. Her verbal communication skills are excellent. I would highly recommend Renée and the iWAM concept as I have personally experienced the great benefit for myself and also my team since completing.'

>>

'Renée is highly skilled in facilitating training in the affective domain. She treats people as very special individuals and can find the positive slant to all situations. Renée had researched the material extremely well; she was able to use relevant anecdotes and examples, tailoring the sessions to the group. She also incorporates her coaching skills to encourage each person in the group. I would recommend Renée to any organisation looking for a professional facilitator with an excellent insight into business, highly developed organisational skills, outstanding people skills and a relaxed presentation style. She gets the job done with positive results for all. I have been a trainer for many years and I would rate Renée as one of the best corporate trainers I have worked with.'

>>

'Renée, how can I appreciate and acknowledge you for how you helped me change, thank you for being the coach I needed you to be. You helped me make some major shifts in my thinking and I am now living in the benefits of that change right now. Renée, you skilfully took me to a place I KNEW was in me but needed your expertise to help me move to a place I had never been. Through your coaching I dealt with wrong beliefs that were holding me back form experiencing the best life possible and also you gave me a way to conquer fear in my life. Since I took on coaching with you Renée, my income has doubled and I expect it to continue to increase, I am working fewer hours and enjoying so much more of life! – Thank you for being an outstanding coach and being totally committed to my benefit! If I could tell EVERYONE to say yes to you being his or her coach, I would.'

www.ingramcontent.com/pod-product-compliance
Lightning Source LLC
Chambersburg PA
CBHW070406200326
41518CB00011B/2084